ACTING ON HOPE

World War II Black and Minority Veterans

Objects At ACES Veterans Museum

A. V. HANKINS, MD FACP
MSEd MPA

ACTING ON HOPE

World War II Black and Minority Veterans

Objects At ACES Veterans Museum

Paperback ISBN: 978-1-965593-08-0

Published by Cornerstone Publishing

A Division of Cornerstone Creativity Group LLC
Info@thecornerstonepublishers.com
www.thecornerstonepublishers.com

Author's Contact

To book the author to speak at your next event or to order bulk copies of this book, please, use the information below:
gcmedical@aol.com

Printed in the United States of America.

DEDICATION

I dedicate this book to Kedan. The memories of the immense joy your brilliant, though painfully brief stay in this world, brought to me will forever remain fresh.

"I still have a dream, a dream deeply rooted in the American dream; that one day this nation will rise up and live up to its creed, "We hold these truths to be self evident: that all men are created equal." I have a dream ……"

DR. MARTIN LUTHER KING JR

CONTENTS

FOREWORD

This book is a timely and important monument to the heroic efforts and exploits of this country's many Black, Latin, Asian, Jewish, and indigenous men and women veterans of World War II. As Founder and Director of ACES Museum, with locations in Philadelphia, Pennsylvania, and Pontiac, Michigan, the author, Dr. Althea Hankins, promotes the dual mission of preserving their patriotic legacies and supporting their wellbeing as living veterans who have sacrificed so much in service to the United States, and to her democratic ideals and institutions.

Employing the artifacts, documents, objects of memorabilia, and oral historical narratives at her museum collection, Dr. Hankins brings to life the wartime experiences and exploits of many well-known service personnel, and the significant events of the time in the world's history. The stories she relays of the courage, and of the sacrifices made by individuals who faced racism and sexism at home, even as they supported the Allied movement to defeat fascism, are both important aspects of history, as well as an urgent reminder that their work represents an ongoing struggle that still resonates today. The book urges us not to take the work of this generation for granted, and to strive to continually rediscover history and honor it in each of our actions today. Ultimately, this book will take its pride of place on the library shelves of those American institutions that hold our veterans in the highest esteem, and in the personal libraries of all those who revere our past military history. Happy reading.

TUOMI JOSHUA FORREST
Executive Director
Historic Germantown
Philadelphia, Pennsylvania.

ACKNOWLEDGMENTS

I acknowledge, with profound gratitude, the efforts of William Broyles Jr. Archivist, and Dr. Aaron Wunsch of the University of Pennsylvania, in making sure that this project eventually saw the light of day. I thank you, from the bottom of my heart, for the blessings you both were to the Parker Hall Project.

INTRODUCTION

History is vital. It tells us about the lives that have been lived, their value, and that what we do has consequences. The Hebrews have special schools that preserve their heritage. The Japanese pay their elders both respect and money to make sure that their culture remains alive. The notion that historical excursions are a waste of time and resources is nothing but a silly and shortsighted perspective. In fact, it is now known that a keen sense and appreciation of historical antecedents can help mitigate the depression and feeling of hopelessness that appears to be so common in young people these days. An understanding of the struggles of their ancestors might actually motivate them to,lead more productive lives. World history is replete with the stories of love, personal endurance, and courage of those who sacrificed their lives to make the world a better place for us all. Those people *acted on hope*. That is why the title of this book is *Acting on Hope*.

World War II will remain one of the most significant events in the annals of mankind. That war changed the lives of people all around the world lived. Women came out, atypically, to work out of necessity, in the process demonstrating both skill and devotion. Black peoples, and those of other minority groups, had to face discrimination and fascism, yet they did so with honor, self-sacrifice, and hard work. America went from a place of segregation and inequality to one of legal desegregation in both civil society and the military. World War II witnessed an escalation of human rights abuses, and the corresponding fight for the restoration of those rights. Blacks people successfully fought *Double Victory Campaigns* against fascism overseas and racism at home. Veterans and their families became noteworthy members of the civil rights movement, notable amongst which were, Medgar Evers and Floyd McKissick. Joe Louis, "the Brown Bomber," one of the greatest and most influential boxers of all time, successfully campaigned for the desegregation of Army buses, and saved Jackie Robinson, the professional baseball player, from being court-martialed. Robinson continued the civil rights struggle and became the first African American to play in Major League Baseball (MLB) in the modern era. Senator Daniel Inouye championed human rights as a Japanese American veteran whose family was placed in internment while he served in World War II. The Japanese would not receive due process until years later when a law was passed to compensate them for loss of liberty and property.

Another veteran, Cesar Chavez, would form a union for migrant workers. He helped to address the plight of the migrant worker and the need for basic human decency, the right to work in a safe environment, fair compensation, and due process before penalization of any sort. Tommy David Hankins was at the forefront of the struggle to establish the United Auto Workers. This union championed the fair treatment of the working class and assisted in the evolution of a middle class. Workers could now directly benefit from the gains of the auto industry, and were now entitled to benefits such as workman's compensation when injured on the job, and a living wage. Manuel Lorenzo was a Puerto Rican who was among thousands that were recruited to fight in World War II but were denied their benefits. He fought and won the victory for all war-related literature to be also published in the Spanish language.

Women were allowed to volunteer for service during World War II. However, Black, Native American, Hispanic and Asian women would face racism as well as sexism.

Fascism dictates how the society must work. It limits the economy and severely constrains opportunities. Fascism dictates how you dress, where you go, how much money you can make, when you can talk, and what you can say. The laws are broad and the power of the dictator is absolute. The chance for trial in which evidence. The police-military, which is the enforcement tool of this form of government, has unfettered authority to kill. They have the authority to torture. Crime against the state is any crime the state says is a crime. Against this backdrop, Black people in the United States experienced full-scale discrimination, lynching, and other atrocities because of the color of their skin and the racist policies that had been in place since the days of slavery.

Yet, there was a difference between the democracy of United States and the fascist governments. The Constitution of the United States says, *"all men are created equal."* In the words of Tommy D. Hankins, a World War II Army veteran of the special forces, *"Our goal was to make sure that the Constitution was followed. This could not have been done if Hitler were also ruling America. This is why we fought, and this is why we won both battles."* Although African Americans have been victims of racial oppression throughout the history of the United States, they have always been patriotic to the nation, especially during wartime. It was during World War II that legal integration took place in the armed forces, even though there were also segregated units. Segregated black units, including the Tuskegee Airmen's 99th Fighter Squadron, fought with distinction. For their wartime heroic feats, they received a distinguished unit citation, several Silver Stars, 150 flying crosses, 14 Brooks Brown stars comp, and 744 air medals. The 761st Tank Battalion fought in the European Theater of Operations. It was the only all-black unit that received the Presidential Unit Citation. They fought for 183 continuous days, conducted over 30 major assaults, held the Germans at bay, and saved countless civilians.

ACES Museum inspired this book. It is a historically unique center of memorabilia for Black and minority veterans of World War II and their families. I had established my medical practice in a building located at 5801-03 Germantown Avenue, Philadelphia. Sometime later, a fortuitous meeting with an entire stranger led me to the astonishing discovery that 5801-03 Germantown Avenue, Philadelphia, was actually the location of the historically-significant *Parker Hall,* an integrated social hall that served as a USO-like facility during World War II for African-American soldiers and their families. After my momentous discovery of Parker Hall, I established ACES Museum to honor Black and Minority veterans of World War II at 5801-03 Germantown Avenue, Philadelphia, and the museum now occupies the upper floor of the historic building.

Remarkably, the Philadelphia Historical Commission, pursuant to its objectives of safeguarding the city's unique heritage and wealth of cultural resources, both to promote economic development, and to foster civic pride, designated the property at 5801-03 Germantown Avenue as historic, and listed it on the Philadelphia Register of Historic Places, in accordance with the City's historic preservation ordinance, Section 14-1000 of the Philadelphia Code.

The vision for ACES Museum is a grand reflection of the sacrifice and exploits of Black people and minorities during World War II. We intend to comprehensively renovate Parker Hall such that the museum will become an international mecca of sorts at which the story of the *Double Victory Campaigns* will be told with unique and exciting clarity. Representations of the Black, Hispanic, Native American, and other Minority experiences will reflect the 1940s WWII environment. Selected artifacts will have the seven-stage unique analysis of *item, production, material composition, historical implication, historical social impact, current social impact, and future implications.* This will allow ACES Museum to rank at par with the Harvard University Museum and its other peers. This will also help create employment opportunities in the areas of *data collection, artifact acquisition, and unique abstract learning* through the tours. Interactive quarterly updated kiosks will keep the museum on the cutting edge of knowledge, while providing webmaster experiences for students.

The museum will also promote science education, college preparation and job readiness. *Educational Enhancement Programs (EPP)* have been providing job, science and historical programs at ACES Museum since 2004. Our programs have an 85% success rate. The adult job training, apprentice section, Reading Rangers, and the children's experience THEM and STEM, will all be enhanced to provide greater opportunities for learning. The Reading Rangers, in particular, will involve additional training and experiences in media arts, software production, mobile apps, computer games and stimulation programs.

Right from its inception, ACES Museum has attracted and assisted Veterans in need. In 2009, ACES Museum was officially certified by the City of Philadelphia as a VSO. Notably, our work with

Vietnam Veterans has commendably earned us the 800-pound *Vietnam Memorial Plaque.* Our expansion and renovation project will accord us the needed luxury of a full-time representative to provide Veterans the services they request of us. The items on display at the museum, and which are, across-board, adequately presented in this book, address the objects themselves, and their possible social impact during World war II. In keeping with the standards at Harvard University, museums are meant to have social and historical relevance and not just be storage warehouses for artifacts. ACES Museum was created not only to highlight the role of Black veterans in World War II, but also to be a place where the efforts and sacrifices of Black and minority veterans of World War II can be truly celebrated. It tells a comprehensive story of the men and women who fought for democracy at home and abroad. They believed in the concept that all men are created equal and that the constitution of the United States of America totally validates that philosophy. It just had to be expanded to truly include all races, sex, and creed. Our heroic veterans were acting on hope. This book is written to celebrate and eulogize that hope.

ALTHEA HANKINS, MD FACP MSEd MPA

Founder & CEO

ACES Museum,

Philadelphia, Pennsylvania

MAJOR CHARITY ADAMS

Major Charity Adams. 6888th Central Postal Directory Battalion

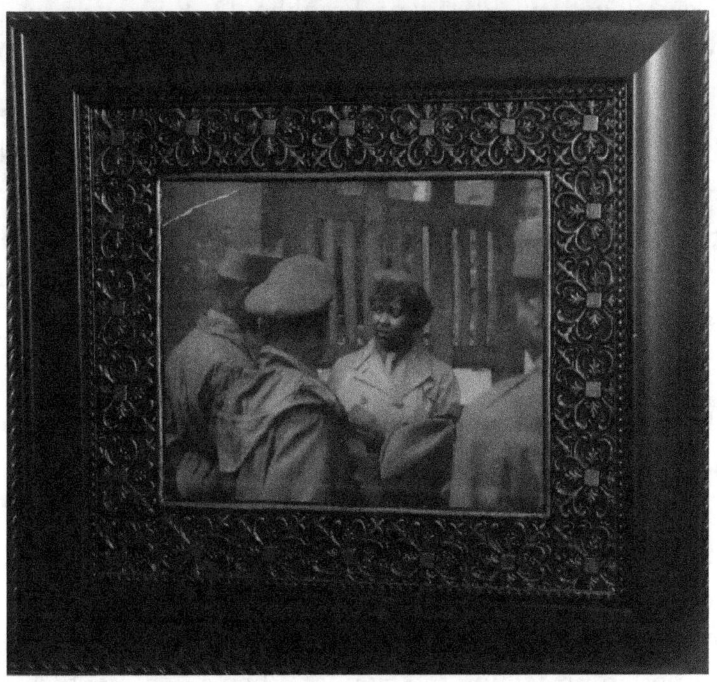

During World War II, sitting in aircraft hangars at Birmingham, England, were millions of undelivered pieces of mail and packages. No mail was being delivered and Army officials reported that a lack of reliable mail was hurting morale. It was predicted that it would take six months to clear the backlog in England, but who was up for the task?

In November 1944, African American women; 824 enlisted and thirty-one officers, were recruited from the Women's Army Corps, the Army Service Forces, and the Army Air Forces to form the 6888th Central Postal Directory Battalion, or the "Six Triple Eight." It would be the first and only all-female African American battalion to be deployed overseas during World War II.

The Women's Army Corps (WAC) of the U.S. Army was created by a law signed by President Franklin D. Roosevelt in 1943. The WAC was converted from the non-military Women's Army Auxiliary Corps, which was created in 1942. First Lady Eleanor Roosevelt and civil rights leader Dr. Mary McLeod Bethune successfully advocated for the admittance of Black women as enlisted personnel and officers in the WAC. The Black 6888th Postal Battalion was given the assignment of correctly processing one million pieces of backlogged mail that was stored in England. They created a new tracking system and processed an average of 65,000 pieces of mail per shift, clearing the six-month backlog of mail in three months. The women adopted the motto of, *"No mail, low morale,"* as they were providing the support of linking service members with their loved ones back home.

Major Charity Adams was the head of the battalion and she stood her ground in protecting the troops. When a General threatened to replace her with a White First Lieutenant to "show" her how to command, she replied, *"Over my dead body, sir!"* The general rescinded the court martial when he realized just how efficient the 6888 were. They were so successful in England that the 6888 was sent to France. Major Charity Adams was promoted to Lieutenant Colonel upon her return to the U.S. The accomplishments of the 6888th in Europe encouraged the General Board of the United States Forces European Theater to acknowledge the Women's Army Corps vital role in the service.[1]

---

1   https://history.army.mil/html/topics/afam/6888thPBn/index.html

AIRPLANE INSTRUMENT

1940 Airplane Salvage. Women's Airforce Service Pilots (WASP)

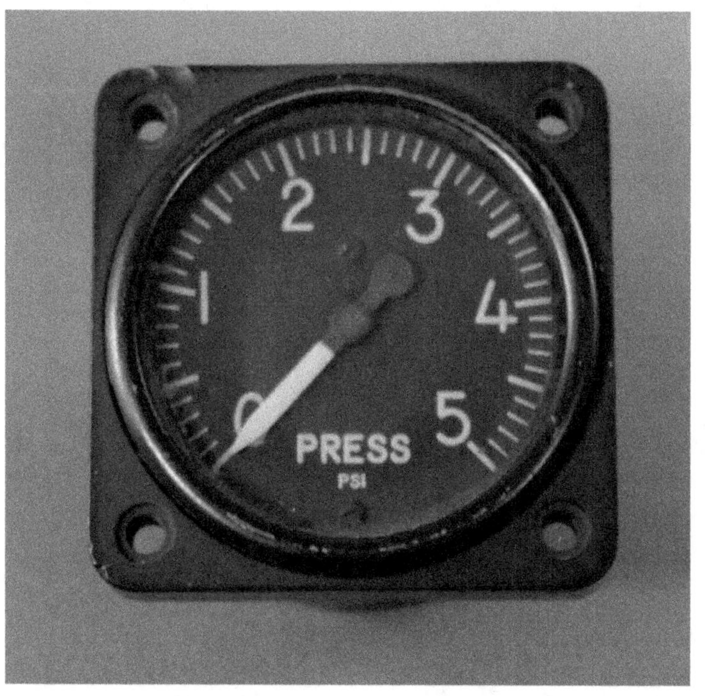

During World War II, in 1942, a critical need for pilots left the door open for experienced women pilots to fly noncombat missions. The Women's Airforce Service Pilots (WASPs) were created from other civilian units. The WASPs were civilian women pilots who were attached to The United States Army Air Force to fly military non-combat missions. Women Airforce Service Pilots (WASP), had 1,100 civilian women with flight duties during World War II. The Women Airforce Service Pilots (WASP) were the first women to fly U.S. military aircraft. In addition to ferrying and delivering supplies, they also performed check flights, put flying time on new engines, towed targets for gunnery practice, flew tracking missions, and instructed male pilot cadets.

The WASP were part of the 350,000 females that served with the Armed Forces in America and abroad during World War II. The WASPs existed from 1942 to 1944. They flew over a million miles in service of the war and used 12,000 military planes. The WASP arrangement with the US Army Air Force ended on December 20, 1944. They were recognized as Veterans for their service to the country in 1977. [2] [3]

---

2   www.britannica.com/topic/Women-Airforce-Service...

3   https://waspmuseum.org/

AFRICAN TROOPS

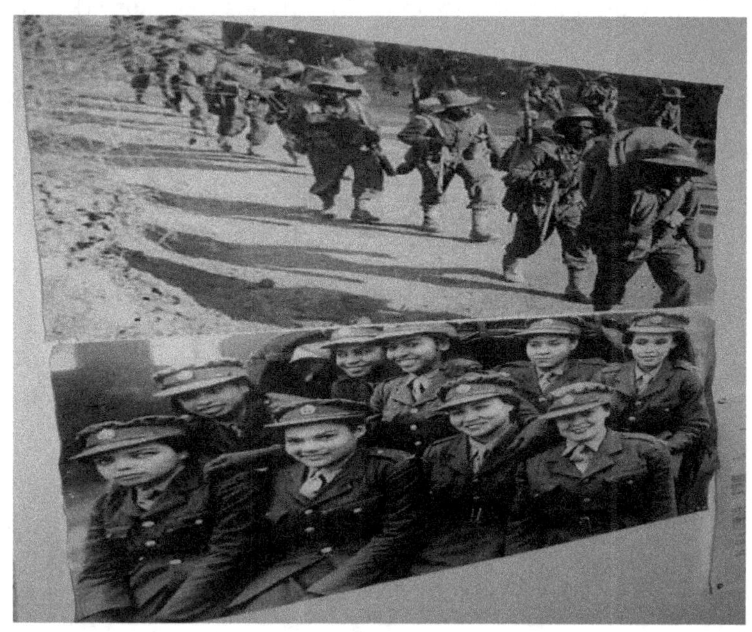

African Troops in World War II generally fought under a British banner. For Africans, World War II actually started in 1935, and not 1939. Italian dictator, Benito Mussolini, ordered troops into Ethiopia. People of the country were instructed to revolt against their Emperor, Haile Selassie. The Italian Army was overwhelming because they used hundreds of tons of chemical weapons on the Ethiopians. Black African soldiers fought in the Army, Air Force and Navy. They joined the East African campaign, which was mainly fought by the Allies of World War II, mainly the British Empire. The British India, Ugandan Protectorate, Kenya, Somaliland, West Africa, Northern and Southern Rhodesia, Sudan and Nyasaland participated in the War effort. The African troops suffered a loss of at least 50,000 men. With the invasion of Ethiopia, during which chemical weapons were used, the number of losses, including civilians, would be anything between 300, 000 and 600,000. Under the coordination of U.S. General Dwight D. Eisenhower, the combined British and American forces pressed on with the fight and after the fall of Tunis, the Axis forces in North Africa surrendered on May 13, 1943. 275,000 German and Italian soldiers were taken, prisoner. [4] [5]

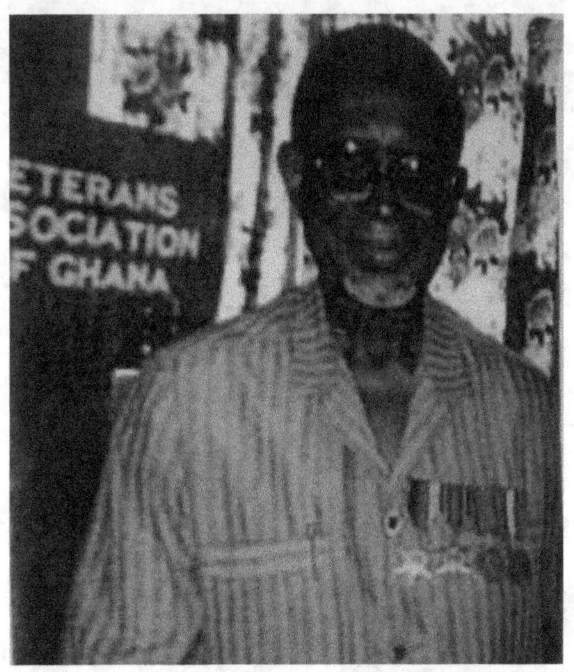

____

4   allthatsinteresting.com/african-soldiers-world-war

5   n.wikipedia.org/wiki/East_African_Campaign...

AIR FORCE GOGGLES

Willa Brown

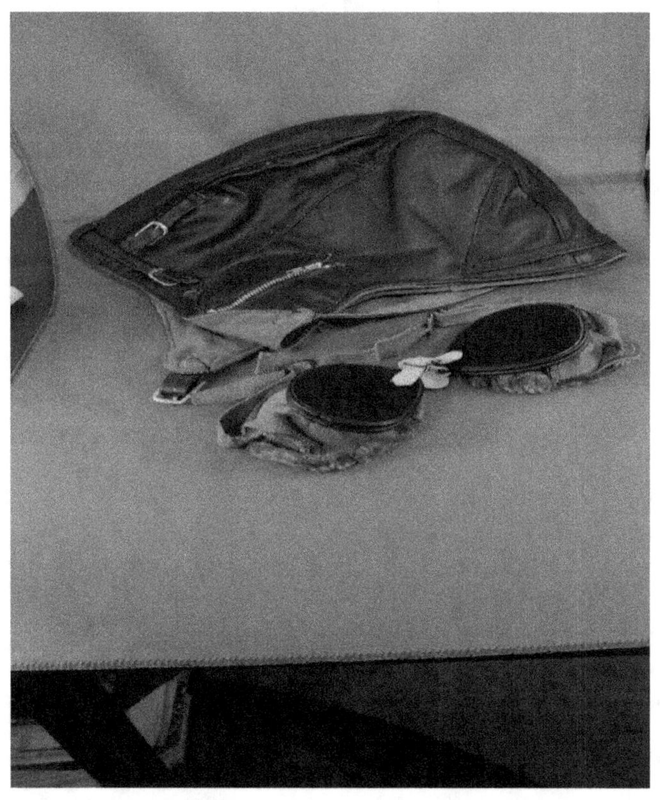

Willa Brown was a pre-World War II Aviator. She earned a Bachelor's degree from Indiana State Teachers College and a Master's degree in business from Northwestern University. In 193, she earned a Masters Mechanic Certificate from Curtiss Wright Aeronautical University, and in 1937 she became the first African American in the U.S. to earn a commercial pilot's license.

Ms. Brown and her husband, Cornelius Coffey, a flight instructor, confounded the Cornelius School of Aeronautics, the first black-owned private flight training academy.

Brown also founded the National Airmen's Association of America. By 1941, Ms. Brown had trained hundreds of men and women, including the Tuskegee Airmen, a group of African American military pilots, fighter and bomber, and airmen who fought in World War II. They formed the 332nd Fighter Group and the 447th Bombardment Group of United States Army Air Forces (USAAF). In 1941, Ms Brown became the first African American officer in the U.S. Civil Air Patrol (CAP). Brown remained politically active, fighting for racial and gender integration in the U.S and Army Air Corps. In 1972, in recognition of her contributions to aviation, Ms. Brown was appointed to the Federal Aviation Administration (FAA) Women's Advisory Board. [6]

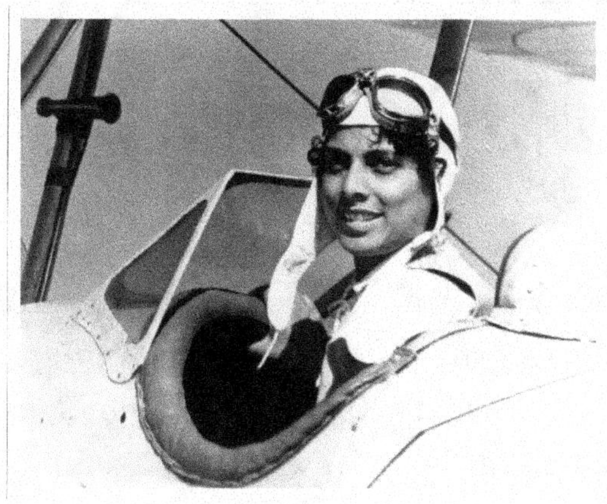

---

6   https://pioneersofflight.si.edu/content/willa-brown-

JOSEPHINE BAKER

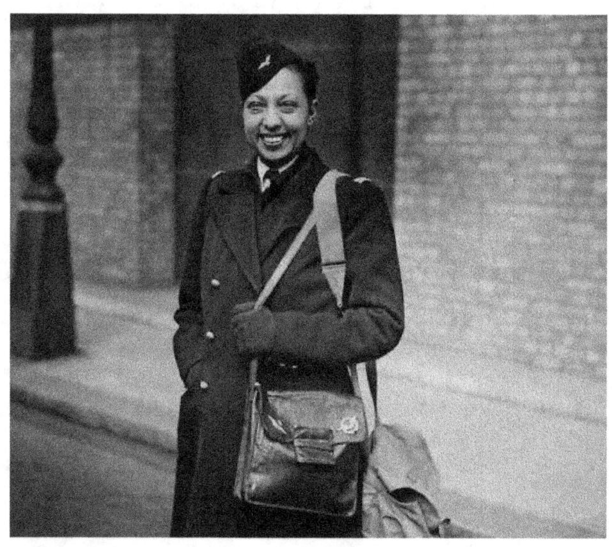

Josephine Baker was an American who became a French citizen because of racial prejudice in America. She graduated from being just a talented dancer to a stage singer and an international star. She was the first black woman to star in a feature film. She was also a recording artist, and a headliner in New York's Ziegfeld Follies. Baker, who refused to perform for segregated audiences in the United States, is noted for her contributions to the Civil Rights Movement. In 1968, she was offered unofficial leadership in the movement in the United States by Coretta Scott King, following Martin Luther King Jr's assassination. After thinking it over, Baker declined the offer out of concern for the welfare of her children.

Ms. Baker was also a spy for the Maquis during World War II.

The Marquis was a group of freedom fighters against German domination. She was a crack shot, but her primary job was to deliver information. The information was written in invisible ink and she would carry it across borders while touring. Ms. Baker was arrested several times but was able to maintain a haven for members of the Resistance. In addition to her work as a spy, Baker volunteered for the Red Cross as a nurse. She was also a pilot, delivering supplies for the fighters in her private plane. She entertained French and Allied Troops. Ms. Baker was awarded multiple medals in France for her dangerous work in World War II. She returned to America and marched for Civil Rights with Dr. Martin Luther King in the 1960s. [7] [8]

-----

7   https://selfrescuingprincesssociety.blogspot.com/2017/06/josephine-baker-world-war-ii-spy.html

8   https://historynewsnetwork.org/article/170603

BARRAGE BALLOON MANUAL

The 320 Barrage Balloon Battalion

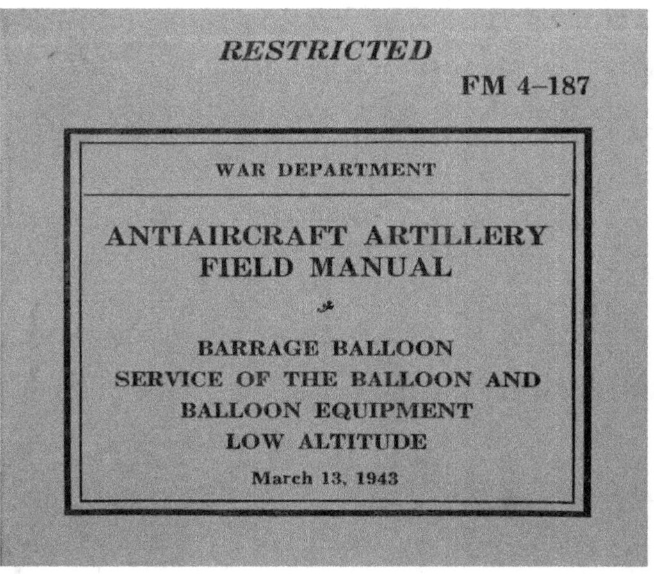

When the United States entered the war, there was a need to train men 18 to 65 years of age. Over 10 million men were inducted into the military while the elective Training and Service Act was in effect from 1940 to 1947. Volunteers came from a wide variety of sources and male volunteer registration was at 37%. All women that served volunteered. Individualized instruction had to be completed on a mass level. Data was originally presented in book form, and there were several manuals. One of the manuals was the *Barrage Balloon Manual.* The soldiers were trained for four weeks and then sent for additional individual training depending on their assignment. The 320 Balloon Battalion was trained for overseas assignments. The Battalion was one of several Battalions trained to handle massive balloons. These balloons were used to stop planes from landing and so they could not fly close enough to their targets. The 320th Barrage Balloon Battalion was sent to Europe and served on the Omaha and Utah beaches during the D-Day invasion, and was in France for 150 days. The 320th Battalion protected American and Allied ships, soldiers, and supplies from German aircraft. For their work on Omaha beach, the Battalion received a commendation from the Supreme Commander of the Allied Expeditionary Forces in Europe, General Dwight D. Eisenhower. [9] [10]

---

9   https://msu.edu/~sleightd/trainhst.html

10   htps://airandspace.si.edu/stories/editorial/protecting-beaches-balloons-d-day-and-320th-barrage-balloon-battalion

BASIC FIELD MANUAL

761 Tank Battalion

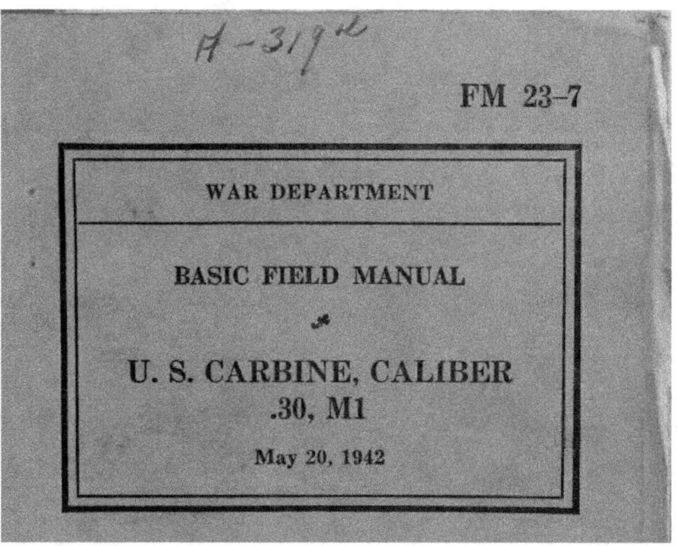

The 761 Tank Battalion became the first black tank battalion to see combat during World War II. They were called the Black Panthers and fought in France, Belgium, and Russia. Their field assignment allowed George S. Patton's troops to enter Germany.

The 761 Tank Battalion was formed in the spring of 1942 and had 30 black officers, six white officers, and 676 enlisted men. This majority-black military unit was known by the nickname "Black Panthers" in reference to the panther patches they wore on their uniforms and their fierce fighting ability. While other units fought for weeks, the 761 Battalion served for over 183 consecutive days. The Panthers were also part of the Allied forces that liberated a concentration camp. The Army awarded the unit four campaign ribbons. In addition, the men of the 761 Battalion received a total of 11 Silver Stars, 69 Bronze Stars and about 300 Purple Hearts. Back at home, though, the surviving members of the battalion returned from Europe to a still-segregated nation. [11]

---

11 history.com/news/761st-tank-battalion-black-panthers-liberators-battle-of-the-bulge

BATTLE OF THE BULGE

Benjamin Berry

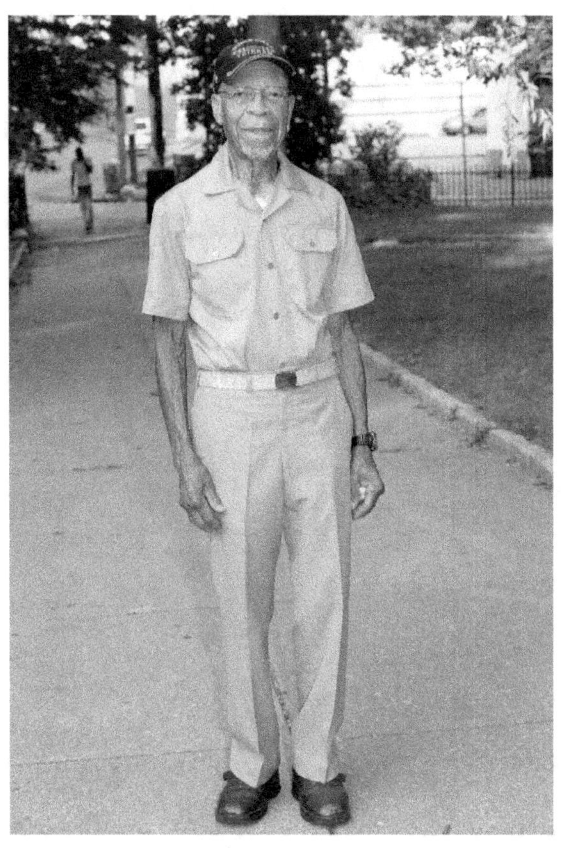

Benjamin Berry was a black soldier who fought in the Battle of the Bulge. He sits on the board of ACES Museum. It was the first time an integrated Army was legally sanctioned. The Battle of the Bulge was the last major German offensive campaign on the Western Front during World War II and took place from December 16, 1944 to January 25, 1945.

The 761st Tank Battalion, the original Black Panthers, were at the major German offensive of the War. Additional Black units to serve in the Battle of the Bulge were the 614th Tank Destroyer, 333rd , 378th , and 969th Field Artillery Battalions, and the 3418th Trucking company (Red Ball Express). Additionally, more than 2,500 Blacks from service units; quartermasters, engineers, and cooks, answered the call for infantrymen.

Benjamin Berry answered the call and continued to fight for civil rights. His most recent accomplishments include the placement of a marker for the colored soldiers of the Civil War at Philadelphia National Cemetery, and helping to preserve Parker hall from unwarranted destruction. [12] [13]

---

12 https://www.history.com/news/761st-tank-battalion-black-panthers-liberators-battle-of-the-bulge

13 www.dogonvillage.com/.../battle_of_the_bulge.htm

BETTY BOOP

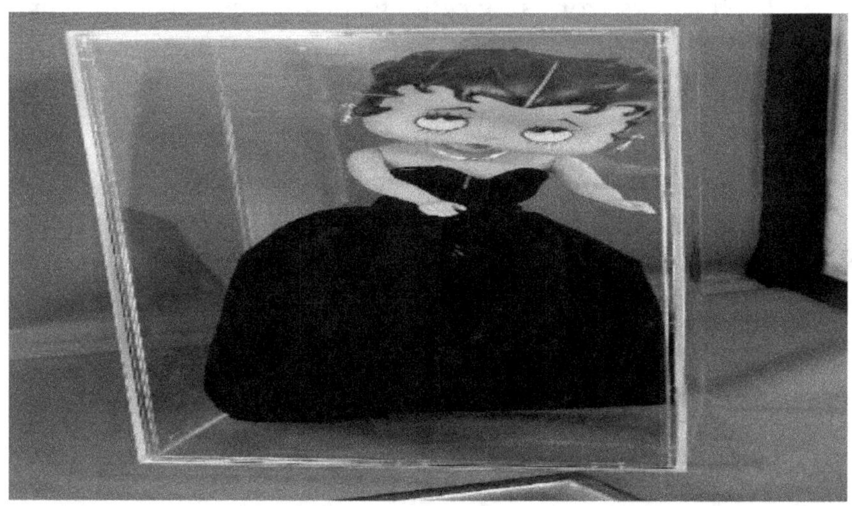

Betty Boop was a cartoon character of the 1930s era, and became extremely popular in the 1940s. In the 1930s she was black and danced with Popeye, the sailor man.

The Black Baby Esther was a popular act at the Cotton Club in Harlem. She sang "boop-boop-a-doops" and other scat sounds. Initially, Betty Boop was black and danced with Popeye in the Sailor Man series. In the video of the cartoon series, it illustrated an integrated dance scene.

Ms. Boop would later be transformed into a white woman by the "discoverers." She became a million-dollar enterprise, while Baby

Esther was neither acknowledged nor compensated. Ms. Esther and her legendary singing act are remembered with the Harlem Renaissance, the preserved videos of Popeye, and Betty Boop in a dress. [14] [15]

____

14   https://www.blackhistory.com/2018/05/real-betty-boop-black-woman-baby-esther-whitewashed.html#:~:text=The%20Real%20Betty%20Boop%20Was%20a%20Black%20Woman...,sin

15   https://www.britannica.com/topic/Betty-Boop

BLACK MEDAL OF HONORS WINNERS OF WORLD WAR II

Picture from the Pentagon Washington, DC - Medal of Honor Recipients

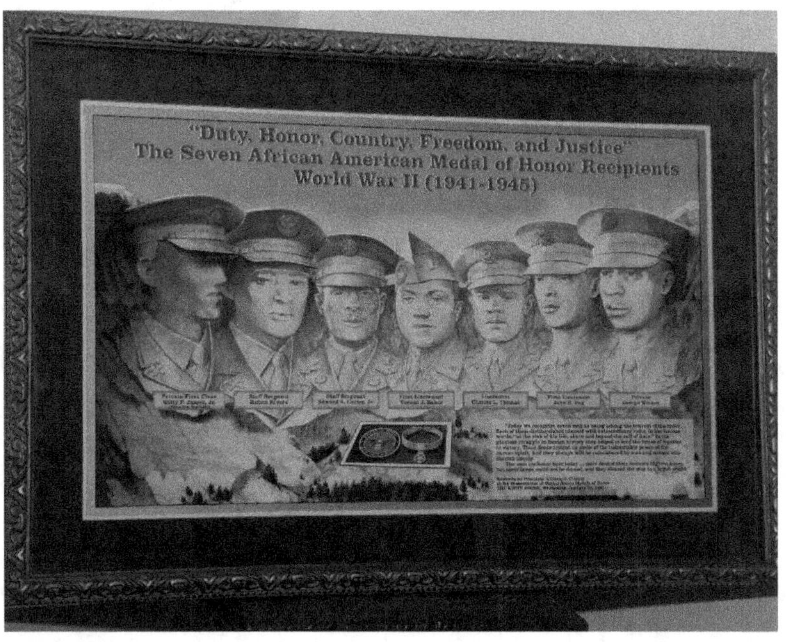

In 1997, following an enabling legislation, President Bill Clinton presented Medals of Honor to African American Veterans who had earlier been denied the honors due to racial disparity during World War II.

The awardee's summary of citations were as follows:

- First Lieutenant Vernon J. Baker. Attacked machine guns and protected wounded personnel.

- Staff Sergeant Edward A. Carter, Jr. Led assaults on tanks and received valuable information.

- First Lieutenant John R. Fox. Stayed in a town in Italy to coordinate fire against the Germans.

- Private First-Class Willy F. James, Jr. Drew fire, exposed enemy fire, and then led the assault.

- Staff Sargent Ruben Rivers. Wounded, yet advanced his tank against a German tank and protected the soldiers.

- Captain Charles L. Thomas. Remained in command while still wounded, making sure antitank guns were in place.

- Private George Watson. Drowned while saving capsized soldiers. [16]

---

16 http://www.history.army/moh.html#FOX

BLACK NURSES

National Archives

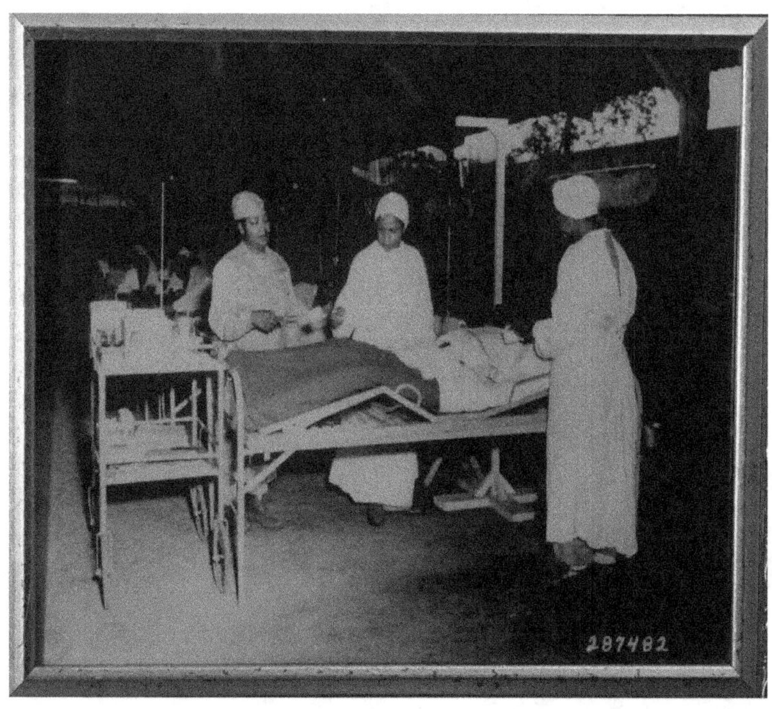

Black nurses served in the Army Nurse Corps when the opportunities became available. In World War II, from 1941 to 1944, they could only be found in segregated units. Their recruitment was limited until there were civilian outcries and a personal plea from First Lady Eleanor Roosevelt. Even at that, the black nurse's duties were restricted to serving black soldiers and German prisoners of war. Instructively, those prisoners were often granted privileges even those Black nurses did not enjoy.

Black nurses cared for troops in 1943 in Liberia, Burma, and England. By the end of the war, Black nurses had served in Africa, England, Burma, and the Southwest Pacific. In 1945 there were 300 Black nurses in the army. These days, African Americans make up 17% of the Army Nurse Corps. [17] [18]

---

17 https://blackthen.com/black-nurses-serving-in-the-military-during-world-war-ii/

18 https://history.army.mil/books/wwii/72-14/72-14.HTM

BLACK ROSIE - ROSIE THE RIVETER

Black Rosies: The Forgotten African American Heroines of The World War II Homefront

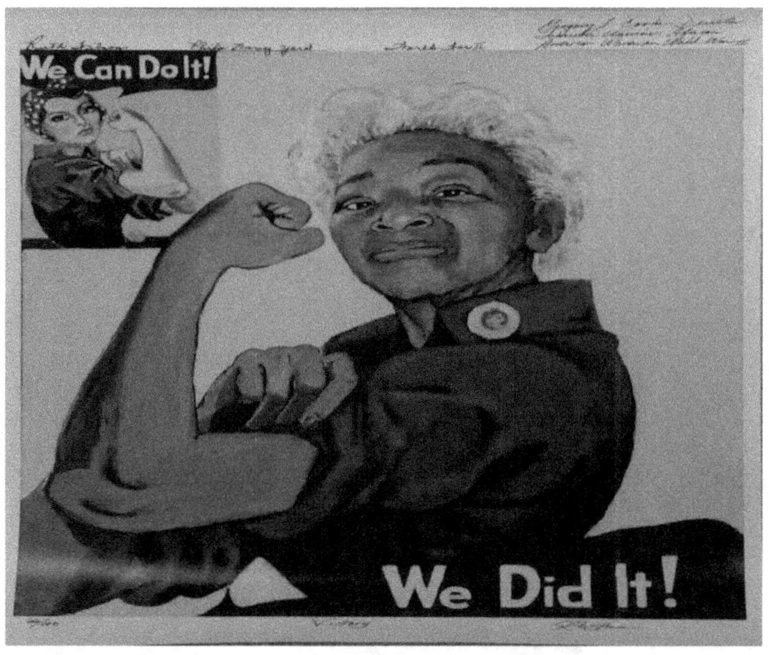

From shipyards to factories to government administrative offices, Black women worked to battle authoritarianism abroad and racism at home. Many men were mandatorily engaged in military service, leading to a shortage of available laborers, and this created a demand for women workers. Black and minority women were a part of the corps of fabled "Rosies." An estimated 600,000 African American women fled oppressive and often demeaning jobs as domestic servants and sharecroppers. They chose instead to help build airplanes, tanks and ships, thereby contributing their own quota to building America's "arsenal of democracy."

Rosie the Riveter, the steely-eyed World War II heroine with her red bandanna, blue coveralls and flexed bicep, stands as one of America's most indelible military images. That image has come to broadly represent the steadfast African American working woman, and more specifically, the millions of Black female laborers who kept the factories and offices of the U.S. defense industries humming. Yet, what the iconic Rosie image doesn't quite convey is the diversity of that work force, specifically the "Black Rosies" who worked alongside their white counterparts in the war effort. They worked tirelessly in shipyards, factories, and along railroads to fight both the foreign enemy of authoritarianism abroad and the familiar enemy of racism at home. For decades, they received little historical recognition or acknowledgement.

Renowned Philadelphia historian and filmmaker, Gregory S. Cooke, noted that it was pressure that was applied on the government by Mary McLeod Bethune, A. Phillipa Randolph, Eleanor Roosevelt, and a host of others that compelled the President to sign the Fair Hiring Practices Act. [19]

---

19   https://www.phillytrib.com/lifestyle/black-rosies-of-wwii-opened-doors-for-others/article_007f433b-c4d5-5359-8d58-7214c8d70069.html

HUMPHREY BOGART

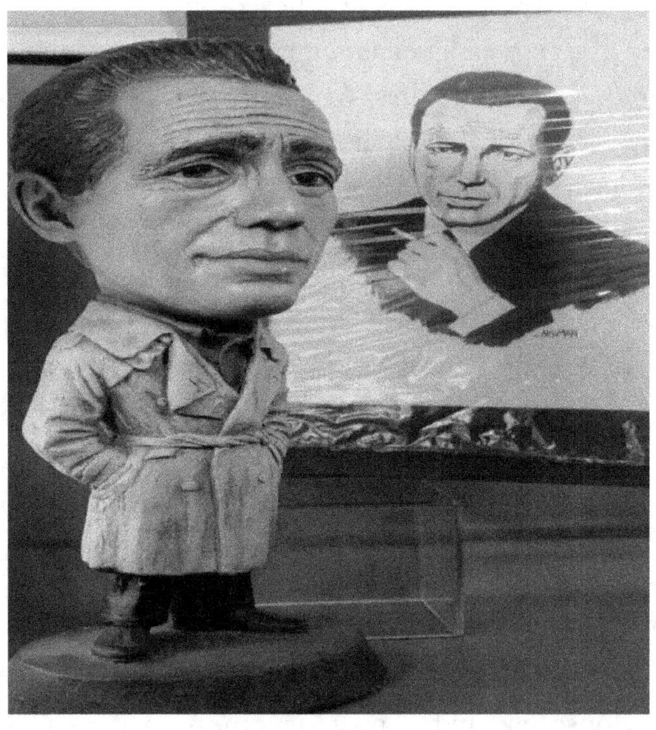

The Hollywood Canteen was started by Hollywood screen legends, John Garfield and Betty Davis. Garfield had a heart condition and could not enlist in the Armed Services. The Canteen operated in Los Angeles and offered food, dancing and entertainment for servicemen of all races. The Hollywood Canteen operated from 1942 and 1945 as a free service for allied servicemen and women in the service. The movie, The Hollywood Canteen, made in 1944, was integrated. Its East Coast Wcounterpart was the New York City–based Stage Door Canteen. It featured Broadway stars and also inspired a film, Stage Door Canteen. At the time the Canteen closed its doors, it had hosted almost three million servicemen. In an era of segregated military service, restrictions on Black people in America, and limitations on blood for Black people at the Red Cross, the Canteen and its integrated and fair policies were a wholesome representation of democracy in action.

Hollywood actually went to *figurative war*. The "Hollywood Unit" made films that became quite iconic. Humphrey Bogart became synonymous with the classic, *Casablanca*, a movie that was timed very well in terms of its relevance to World War II, although viewers today are more likely to identify with the film's romantic tale of love and honor. [20]

____

20   https://en.wikipedia.org/wiki/Hollywood_Canteen

BOOKS

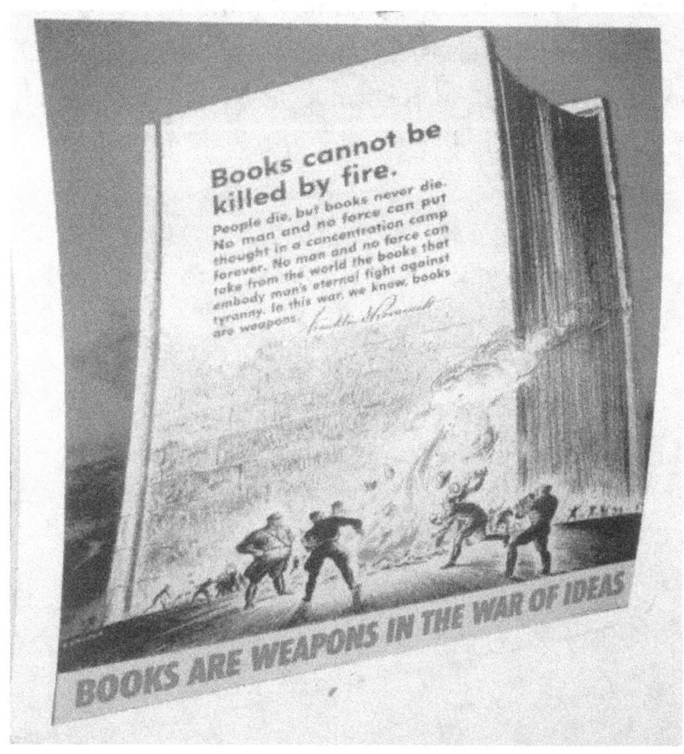

The first target of Adolf Hitler and his Nazi Party were books. This began in 1933, shortly after Hitler seized power in Germany. He ordered any book that did not support his thoughts confiscated and destroyed. Independent thought was considered dangerous. Modern-day equivalents might easily be those who desire to suppress internet access in their countries.

The Nazi book burnings were a campaign that ceremonially burnt books in Nazi Germany and Austria in the 1930s. The books targeted for burning were those viewed as being subversive or as representing ideologies opposed to Nazism. These included books written by Jewish, Communist, Socialist, anarchist, liberal, and pacifist authors. [21] [22]

---

21   http://totallyhistory.com/nazi-book-burnings/
22   Internet Censorship 2020: A Global Map of Internet ...

ARMY BOX - WORLD WAR II

Tommy D. Hankins of The Special Forces

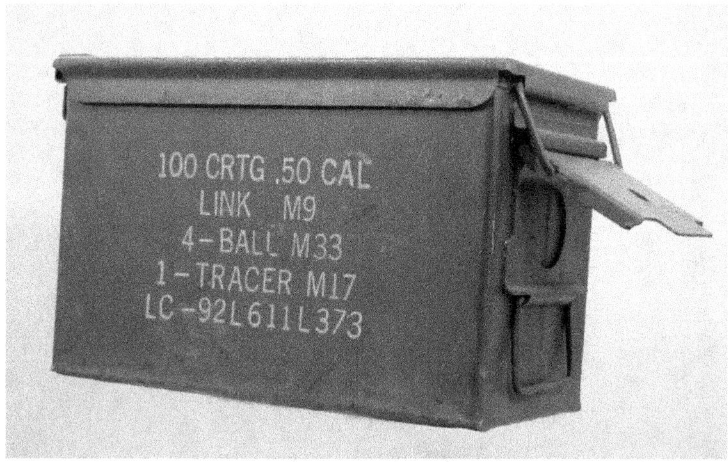

Tommy D. Hankins, who also went by the Muslim name, Dawud Muhammed, served four tours of duty during World War II, a most unusual feat at that time. He was a part of the Black special forces sent to Japan to test the effects of some bombs. Given how patriotic he was, he was questioned as to how he could be so committed to a country that discriminated against him because of the color of his skin. His reply was that the Constitution of the United States states that "all men are created equal." The full version reads, *"We hold these truths to be self-evident, that all men are created equal, that they are endowed by their Creator with certain inalienable rights, that among these are Life, Liberty, and the pursuit of Happiness."*

How true are these words? The truth is simply that America has never been a country where people are truly equal. It is, however, an aspiration to continue to work towards. But, America is not there yet. This box, a relic of World War II, speaks into that hope, and that aspiration. Tommy D. Hankins helped to form the UAW, United Auto Workers. His wife, Gwendolyn Broyles Hankins, was a *Rosie*, and a Civil Rights advocate. When asked how she could marry a Muslim, she replied, "Faith is what you do." They died within months of each other.

BUFFALO PATCH

Buffalo Soldiers (1866-1951)

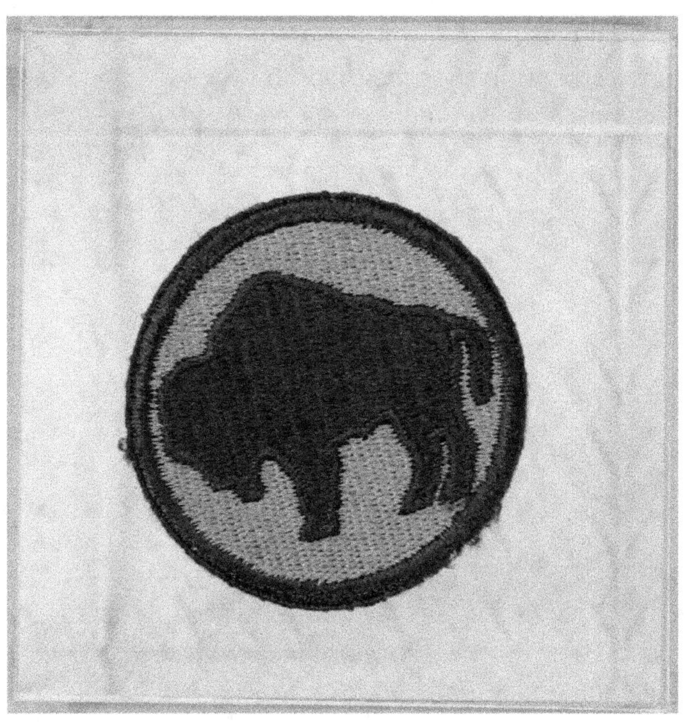

As subjects of both historical study and popular legend, the African American servicemen known as "Buffalo Soldiers" continue to provoke conversations.

The heroism of the soldiers has been celebrated by filmmakers, musicians, and descendants who want to preserve their legacy.

Yet that legacy is a complex one and raises challenging questions about the relationship of the soldiers to the government they served as well as to the native peoples they fought.

These all-black regiments were led mainly by white U.S. Army officers. The three black officer exceptions were West Point graduates Henry O. Flipper, John Hanks Alexander, and Charles Young. These black soldiers helped protect the nation's westward expansion by building roads and participating in significant military actions, such as the Red River War (1874-1875) and the Battle of San Juan Hill during the Spanish American War (1898). The brave men also served among the first national park rangers. Black soldiers used military service as a strategy to obtain equal rights as citizens. Paradoxically, they sought to achieve this by engaging in government-led wars meant to overtake the Southwest and Great Plains from Native Americans.

The Buffalo soldiers built up an impressive record. Of 12,846 Buffalo soldiers who saw action, 2,848 were killed, captured, or wounded. The Buffalo Soldiers broke through the G Line in Italy. They reached their objective, captured or helped to capture nearly 24,000 prisoners and received more than 12,000 decorations and citations for their gallantry in combat. The soldiers of the 92nd Division proved their worth through months of bitter combat in the Italian campaign. Blacks would fight with distinction during the war in other areas, including combat in the Pacific. [23]

---

23 https://www.militarytimes.com/military-honor/black-military-history/2018/02/14/how-the-buffalo-soldiers-helped-turn-the-tide-in-italy-during-world-war-ii/

PAPERWEIGHT

Camp Mackall, North Carolina

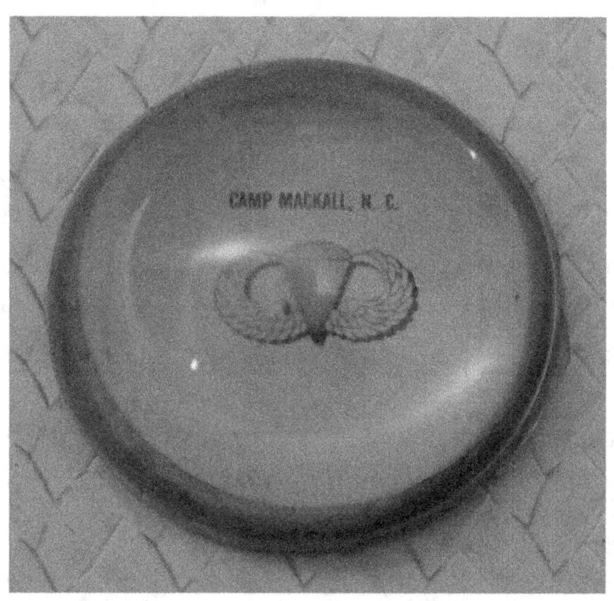

Paperweights are solid objects in standard dimensions of 2.5 and 3.5 inches. These domes are used to accent the enclosed items and are generally used as collectibles. Camp Mackall is located in North Carolina. It began as a separate U.S. Army training base during World War II. Three airborne divisions were formed and trained there from 1943 to 1945.

Initially named Camp Hoffman, the facility was renamed Camp Mackall in honor of Private John Thomas Mackall, a paratrooper. The camp was a marvel of wartime construction, having been converted from 62,000 acres of wilderness to a camp with 65 miles of paved roads, a 1,200-bed hospital, five movie theaters, six huge beer gardens, a complete all-weather airfield with three 5,000-foot runways, and 1,750 buildings in just four months. [24] [25]

---

24   https://arsof-history.org/articles/v3n4_camp_mackall_page_1.html

25   https://www.glasspaperweightfoAboutPaperweightsundation.com/all_about_paperweight.

CANTEEN SHOVEL

Quartermasters Troops and the Red Ball Express

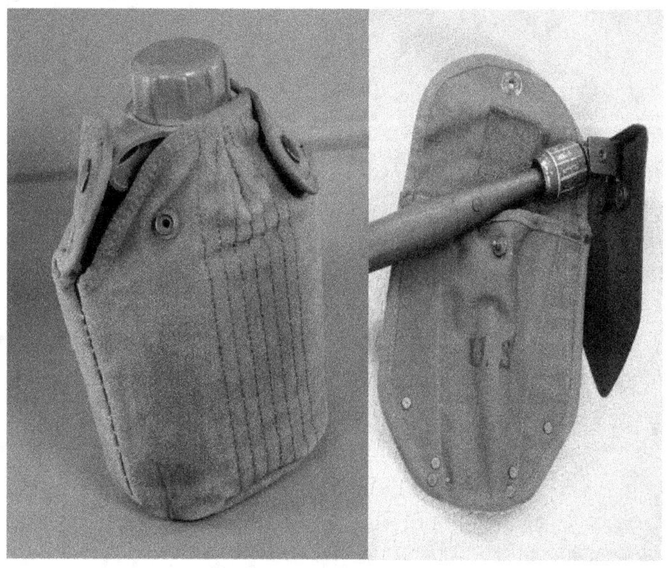

The U.S. Army Quartermaster section is its oldest logistics branch. It was established in 1775. Quartermaster means master of quarters; one who goes ahead to provide lodging. Their job is to provide logistics support for the Army. More than 32,000 officers, officer cadets and key enlisted personnel received their training at the Quartermaster School between July 1, 1940 and December 3, 1945. The physical conditioning of entrants was emphasized, along with rigorous military training. They had to shovel foxholes.

The Red Ball Express was a series of truck convoys that carried supplies for General Patton's Third Army. Through a span of 82 days in 1944, the black soldiers delivered more than 400,000 tons of war materials over 700 miles to the front in a route marked with red balls. Their efficiency prompted a British infantry brigade commander to note, *"Few who saw them will ever forget the enthusiasm of the Negro drivers, hell-bent whatever the risk, to get General George Patton his supplies."* Some also participated in armed combat. Private George Watson was a Black Medal of Honor recipient. He was a quartermaster who gave his life to saving others. [26] [27] [28]

26   https://quartermaster.army.mil/history/u-s-history.com/pages/h1714.html

27   https://qmmuseum.lee.army.mil/WWII/qm_school.htm

28   https://www.dav.org/learn-more/news/2015/black-history-month-2015-remembering-red-ball-express/#

CHRISTMAS BOX

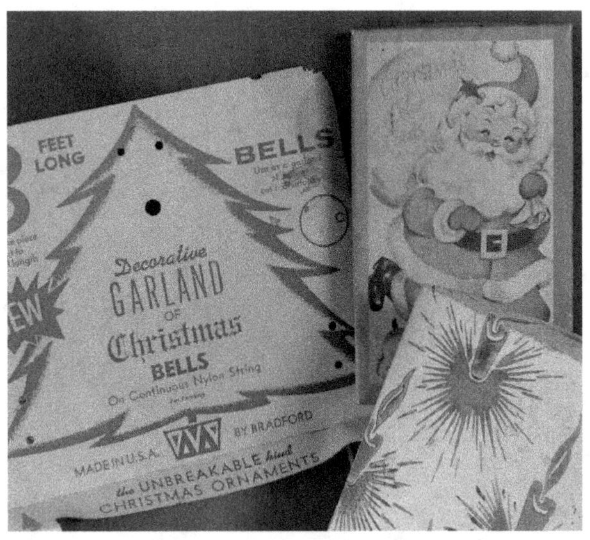

The Buffalo soldiers wanted to fight. The Black community protested for them to get a chance to fight and represent themselves as equal citizens and men during World War II. They were to prove and justify that qualification on a special Christmas Day.

On a certain Christmas Eve, the Fifth Army had called off its Christmas Day assault in Italy. The Buffalo Soldiers were deployed on both sides of the Serchio River and were forced to advance. They faced German mortar and artillery rounds as they moved through more of northern Italy's mountain towns. Before sunrise on the day after Christmas, the Germans attacked the villages just north and east of Gallicano. Many of the Germans were dressed as partisans, making the situation even more confusing and dangerous. Just before noon, the platoons were ordered to evacuate the village, but they were trapped. They managed to hold out until nightfall, but of the 70 Americans involved, only one officer and 17 men managed to fight their way out of the village that night as ordered. Fighter-bombers roared into the valley and hammered Sommocolonia, Gallicano and other front-line areas, and by January 1, the Allies had re-established their original positions. The village was not overtaken due to the determination of the 92nd Infantry and their refusal to surrender during that Christmas or any other period, for that matter. [29]

---

29 https://www.militarytimes.com/military-honor/black-military-history/2018/02/14/how-the-buffalo-soldiers-helped-turn-the-tide-in-italy-during-world-war-ii/

COON CHICKEN POSTER

Segregation and Black Codes

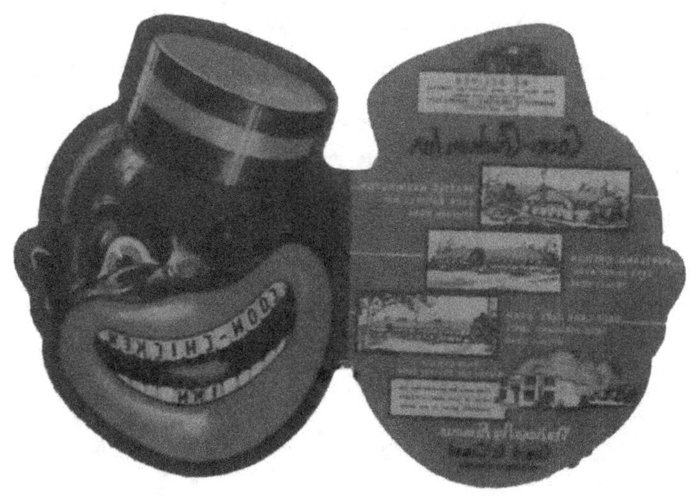

The Jim Crow laws were state and local laws introduced in the Southern United States in the late 19th and early 20th centuries that enforced racial segregation, "Jim Crow" being a pejorative term for an African American. Such laws remained in force until 1965. The Jim Crow laws began as early as 1865, immediately following the ratification of the 13th Amendment, which abolished slavery in the United States. These codes were strict and detailed a legal way to keep black citizens in servitude. The codes appeared throughout the South as a legal way to control how they lived, worked, traveled and were treated in court. They made it legal to seize children for labor purposes.

The post-World War II era saw an increase in civil rights activities in the African American community, focusing on ensuring that Black citizens could vote. This ushered in the civil rights movement, resulting in the removal of Jim Crow laws.

SPECIFICALLY:

- In 1948 President Harry Truman ordered integration in the military.

- In 1954, the Supreme Court ruled in Brown v. Board of Education that educational segregation was unconstitutional.

- 1964, President Lyndon B. Johnson signed the Civil Rights Act, which legally ended the segregation that Jim Crow laws had institutionalized. [30]

---

30   https://www.history.com/topics/early-20th-century-us/jim-crow-laws

DUKE, A WING AND A PRAYER

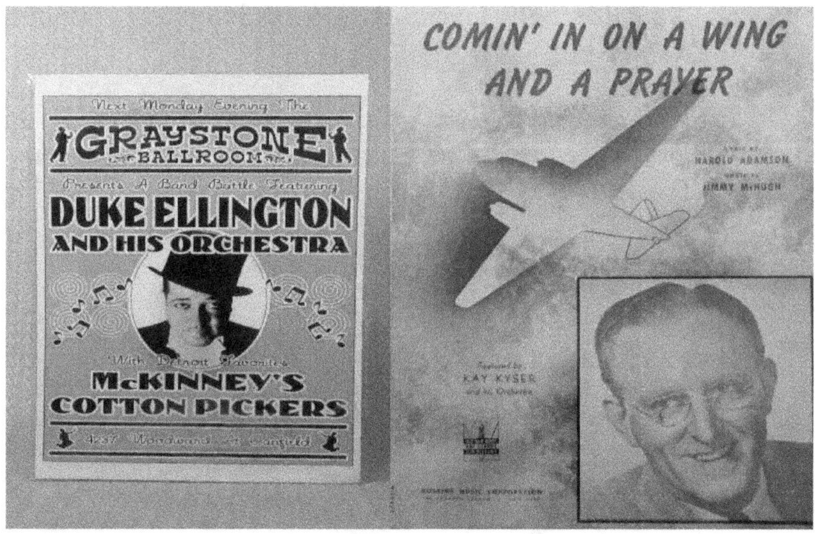

Music played several roles during World War II. 96.2 % of American families had radios, making music a universal commodity. American music featured jazz, which was banned by Germany. Music was a source of inspiration, motivation, and civil rights updates. Some of the music was inspired by the war, as above. Music helped people cope with the stress of the war, and to grieve for their losses. Popular artists included Frank Sinatra, Ella Fitzgerald, the Andrew Sisters and Duke Ellington. Duke Ellington was special. Band leader Edward Kennedy "Duke" Ellington was a musical genius. He composed over one thousand works, traveled all over the world with his band and was featured in motion pictures.

In 1943 Duke Ellington and his band made their debut at Carnegie Hall at the height of World War II. He used his music to promote respect and racial harmony. His longest composition was *Black, Brown, and Beige.* [31] [32] [33]

31   wikipedia.org/wiki/American_music_during.world war II.

32   www.bartleby.com/essay/The-Role-of-Music-during..world war II.

33   lvphil.org/2020/06/the-music-plays-on-duke-ellington-black-brown-and-beige-by-donato-cabr

EAR WARDENS

Hearing Protective Devices Developed During World War II

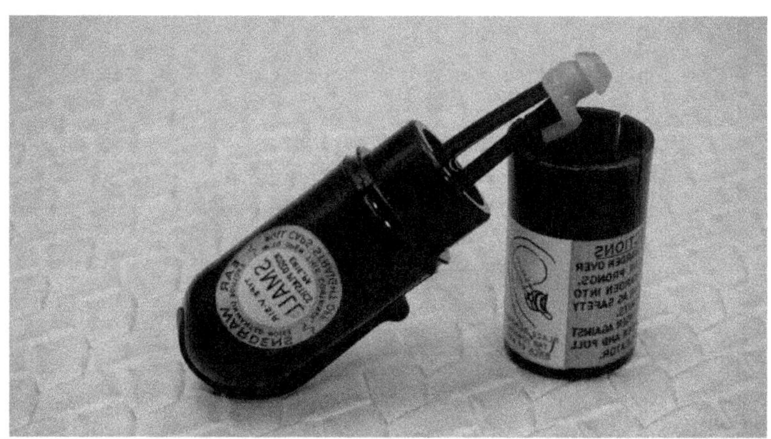

Ear wardens are hearing devices known as HPD. They are worn in or over the ears to protect from hearing loss. There was a 10-20% hearing loss during WWI. A study by the U.S. Army in the 1940s led to a recommendation that gun crews and others exposed routinely to gunfire be provided with hearing protection. The Ear Warden V-51R was developed during the end of World War II. They were produced in different sizes, an innovation of that time period. Hearing rehabilitation was also started in the newly reorganized Veterans Administration.

Hearing loss has become so prevalent that 17 percent of young people between 12 and 19 have some degree of noise-induced hearing loss. They may not realize the issue is permanent and fail to seek help. Any hearing change should be investigated, regardless of age. People should avoid loud noise exposure, use earplugs on noise-canceling headphones. Each of these will reduce sound intensity by 30 decibels. People should also stop smoking to decrease damage to ear hair cells. [34] [35]

---

34   www.ishn.com/articles/106961-tracing-the-origins-of-hearing-protection#:~:text=A%20landmark

35   https://asa.scitation.org/doi/abs/10.1121/1.1917477

FIELD COMMUNICATIONS TELEPHONE

The Marines

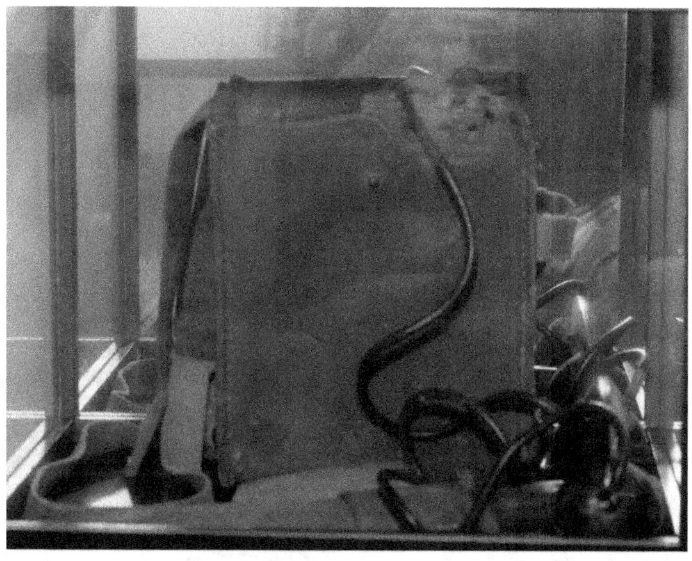

Marines were part of the Naval wing of armed forces. From 1798 to 1942, Black people were denied entrance into the Marines. After Executive Order 8802 forbade racial discrimination, Howard Perry and others joined the Marines and trained at Montford Point, North Carolina. The Black USMC recruits would form the 51st and 52nd Defense Battalions. In total, 19,168 African Americans joined the Marines, about 4% of the USMC's strength.

75% of them performed their duties overseas. About 8,000 black USMC stevedores and ammunition handlers served under enemy fire during offensive operations in the Pacific.

In 1944 the 7th Marines needed help to get their wounded to safety.

The segregated companies of the 16 Marine Field Depot and the 17th Special Seabees volunteered to assist. The counteraction was repulsed and the Black troops received written commendations for their heroic actions. Following the June 1944 Battle of Saipan, USMC General Alexander Vandegrift said of the steadfast performance of the all-black 3d Marine Ammunition Company, *"The Negro Marines are no longer on trial. They are Marines. Period."*

Women have been part of the Marines since 1918. The Marine Corps Reserves had 20,000 women in 225 different jobs in World War II. There were 874 Native American Code talkers in the Marines during World War II. Only white Hispanics were admitted into the Marines at that time. The Marines would not become fully intergraded until 1960. [36] [37]

---

36   https://en.wikipedia.org/wiki/Desegregation_in_the_United_States_Marine_Corps

37   https://marineparents.com/marinecorps/women

FOUR FREEDOMS - BILL OF RIGHTS

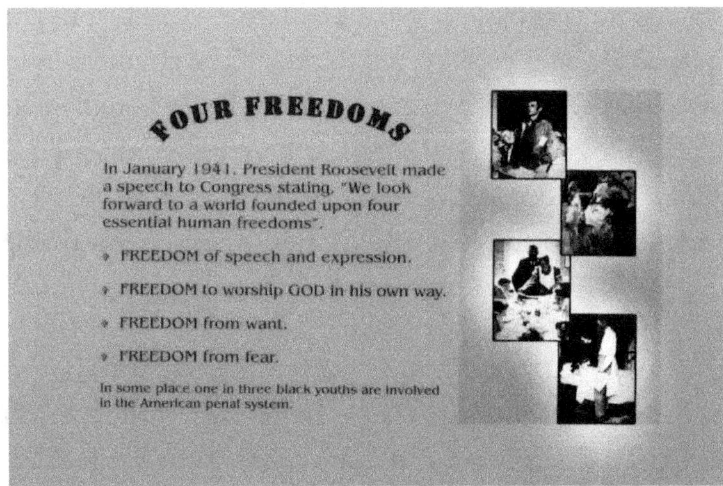

The Four Freedoms were goals articulated US President Franklin D. Roosevelt on Monday, January 6, 1941. In an address known as the Four Freedoms Speech (technically the 1941 State of the Union address), he proposed four fundamental freedoms that people "everywhere in the world" ought to enjoy:

- *Freedom of speech and expression*

- *Freedom of speech*

- *Freedom from want*

- *Freedom from fear*

Constitutional Bill of Rights. The first 10 Amendments to the Constitution.

Amendment 1: Freedom of Religion, Speech, and the Press Congress shall make no law respecting an establishment of religion or prohibiting the free exercise thereof, or abridging the freedom of speech or of the press, or the right of the people peaceably to assemble and to petition the government for a redress of grievances.

Amendment 2: The Right to Bear Arms

A well-regulated Militia being necessary to the security of a free State, the right of the people to keep and bear Arms shall not be infringed.

Amendment 3: The Housing of Soldiers

No soldier shall, in time of peace, be quartered in any house without the consent of the owner, nor in time of war but in a manner to be prescribed by law.

Amendment 4: Protection from Unreasonable Searches and Seizures

The right of the people to be secure in their persons, houses, papers, and effects against unreasonable searches and seizures shall not be violated, and no warrants shall issue but upon probable cause, supported by oath or affirmation, and particularly describing the place to be searched and the persons or things to be seized.

Amendment 5: Protection of Rights to Life, Liberty, and Property

No person shall be held to answer for a capital or otherwise infamous crime unless on a presentment or indictment of a grand jury, except in cases arising in the land or naval forces or in the militia when in actual service in time of war or public danger; nor shall any person be subject for the same offense to be twice put in jeopardy of life or limb; nor shall be compelled in any criminal case to be a witness against himself, nor be deprived of life, liberty, or property without due process of law; nor shall private property be takenmfor public use without just compensation.

Amendment 6: Rights of Accused Persons in Criminal Cases

In all criminal prosecutions, the accused shall enjoy the right to a speedy and public trial by an impartial jury of the state and district wherein the crime shall have been committed, which district shall have been previously ascertained by law, and to be informed of the nature and cause of the accusation; to be confronted with the witnesses against him; to have compulsory process for obtaining witnesses in his favor; and to have the assistance of counsel or his defense.

Amendment 7: Rights in Civil Cases

In suits at common law, where the value in controversy shall exceed twenty dollars, the right of trial by jury shall be preserved, and no act tried by a jury shall be otherwise reexamined in any court of the United States than according to the rules of the common law.

Amendment 8: Excessive Bail, Fines, and Punishments Forbidden

Excessive bail shall not be required, nor excessive fines imposed, nor cruel and unusual punishments inflicted.

Amendment 9: Other Rights Kept by the People

The enumeration in the Constitution of certain rights shall not be construed to deny or disparage others retained by the people.

Amendment 10: Undelegated Powers Kept by the States and the People

The powers not delegated to the United States by the Constitution, nor prohibited by it to the states, are reserved to the states respectively, or to the people. [38] [39]

---

38   https://www.britannica.com/event/Four-Freedoms

39   https://nccs.net/blogs/americas-founding-documents/bill-of-rights-amendments-1-10

FUR AND HATS. 1940

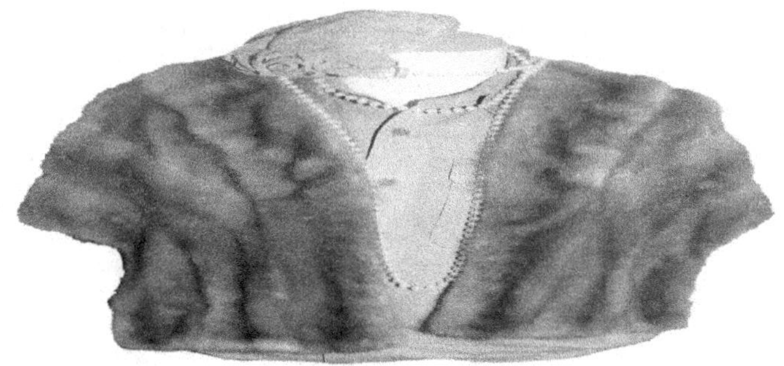

There were many rich and upper middle class women in the Special Operations Executive. They abandoned a life of privilege to assist the French Resistance and fight for freedom from German occupation. S.O.E. was a network of spies and amateurs that wrought havoc on German-dominated Europe. Scores of female operatives worked for the S.O.E. These women were trained to handle guns and explosives, memorize complex codes, organize munitions and supplies drops, endure harsh interrogation, and, in some cases, supervised thousands of men.

They grew from 39 volunteers to a large number that organized D-Day in occupied France. Especially noteworthy were Nancy Wake, who used her wealth to buy ambulances, while she helped allied soldiers and political prisoners in setting up an "underground railway," and Virginia Hall, who was an American and British spy. She mapped drop zones for equipment and soldiers. There was also Inayat Khan, a princess who became the first female radio operator to be sent from the United Kingdom to France in the summer of 1943. Her work as a secret agent became crucial to the war effort's communication. Her last spoken word was "Liberty." [40] [41]

---

40   https://www.thevintagenews.com/2016/10/03/top-five-female-spies-world-war-ii/

41   https://time.com/5892932/a-call-to-spy-real-history/

HARLEM COWBOYS POSTER. 1939

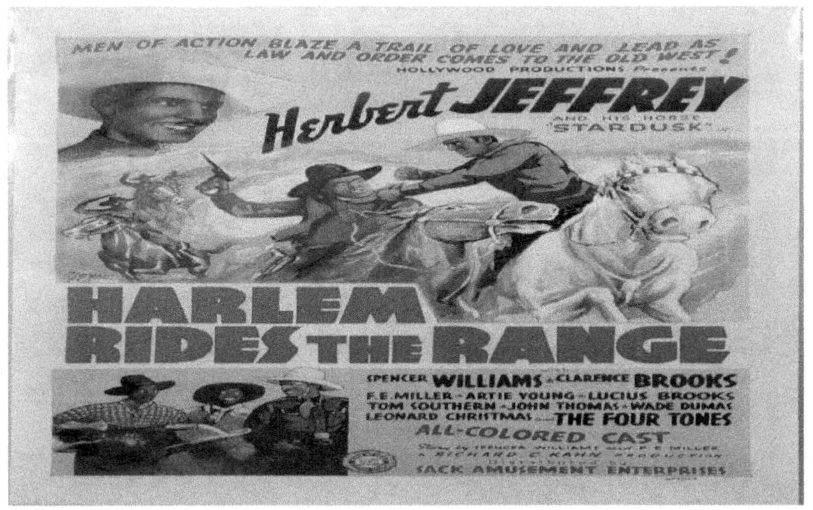

Many freed slave came to the American West to settle. They came for work opportunities and a less segregated environment. Of the 35,000 cowboys in the 1880s, 25% were black. The name "cowboy" was meant to be a derogatory form of a cowhand. Over time, the contribution of Black people to the cowboy culture was ignored by history, and cowboys referred to white males only.

In the 1930s and 1940s, there was a thriving independent Black-owned cinema industry. Blacks were drawn to the independence and success of the Black western experience. The Harlem western experience was actually a mixture of two worlds. The

"Bronze Buckaroo," Herb Jeffries, was a jazz singer and actor who performed with Duke Ellington in a series of all-Black 1930s Westerns. He was known as the only Black-singing cowboy in the movies. [42] [43] [44]

42   https://allthatsinteresting.com/black cowboys#:~:text=%20The%20 Forgotten%20Black%20Cowboys

43   https://atlantablackstar.com/2015/07/24/forgotten-story-americas-black-cowboys/

44   https://www.fesfilms.com/public-domain/black-heritage.html

HELMET

Induction by Race in World War II

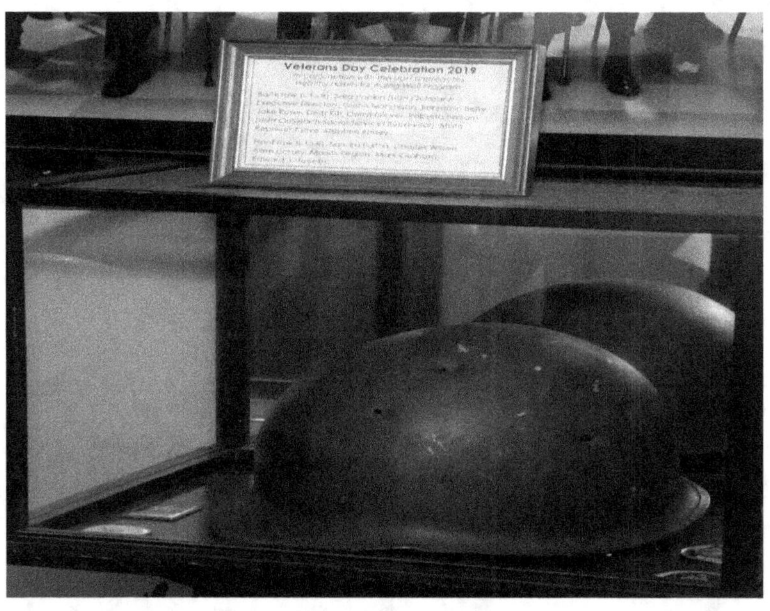

One million African Americans had been inducted as of December 31, 1945. They included:

- 1. 885,945 went into the Army (10.9 %)

- 2. 153,224 into the Navy (10.0%)

- 3. 16,005 into the Marine Corps (8.5%)

- 4. 1,667 into the Coast Guard (10.9%)

Other racial and nationality groups:

- 1. 13,311 Chinese

- 2. 20,080 Japanese
- 3. 1,320 Hawaiians
- 4. 44,000 American Indians
- 5. 11,506 Filipinos
- 6. 51,438 Puerto Ricans

---

45 https://www.history.army.mil/documents/WWII

HOMECOMING. WORLD WAR II

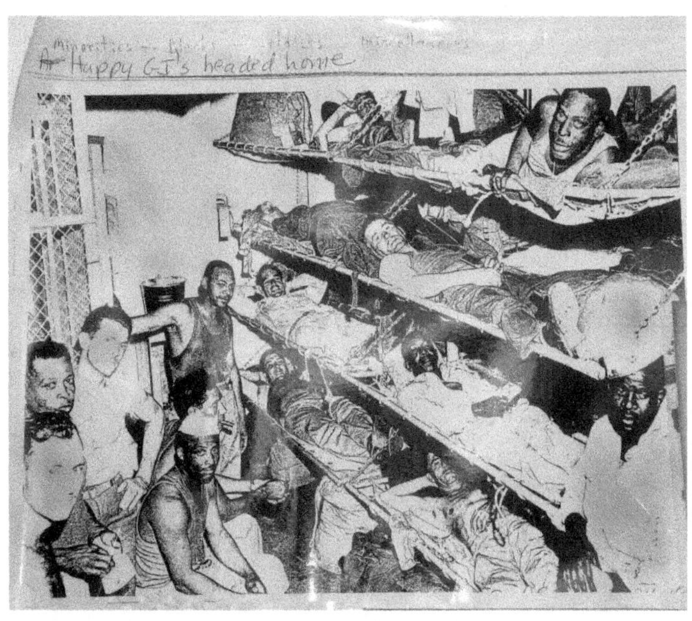

There were different reasons and motivations for being in the military during World War II. Some men were drafted and had no legal choice. Others volunteered for the love of country. Some minorities fought for the right to fight in the War in order to prove that they merited equal rights and could meet the responsibilities that came with them. They believed that a victory against global fascism could help defeat racism in America. They took that strategic approach in the hope that serving in the military would help eliminate racial discrimination and segregation.

Women also enlisted. They shared the same motivation as the men. This included patriotism, opportunity for advancement, but with the added hope that the limited perception of female capabilities would change. Whatever the motivation, minorities faced further discrimination in the US armed forces during World War II. At the start, all military branches were segregated, and women's role was severely restricted. Their valor, however, changed people's minds. Women's opportunities were expanded, and they were able to serve directly with the armed forces rather than being just auxiliaries. The Executive Order 9981 of 1948, signed by President Harry S. Truman, ordered the end of military segregation. Some veterans did not need a legal document during the Battle of the Bulge, including the Tuskegee Airmen and others, to end segregation. They were all Americans and deserved to fight and go home together. [46]

———————

46 https://en.wikipedia.org/wik/Ethnic_minorities_in_the_US_armed_forces_during_World_War_II

HOME DEFENSE GUIDE

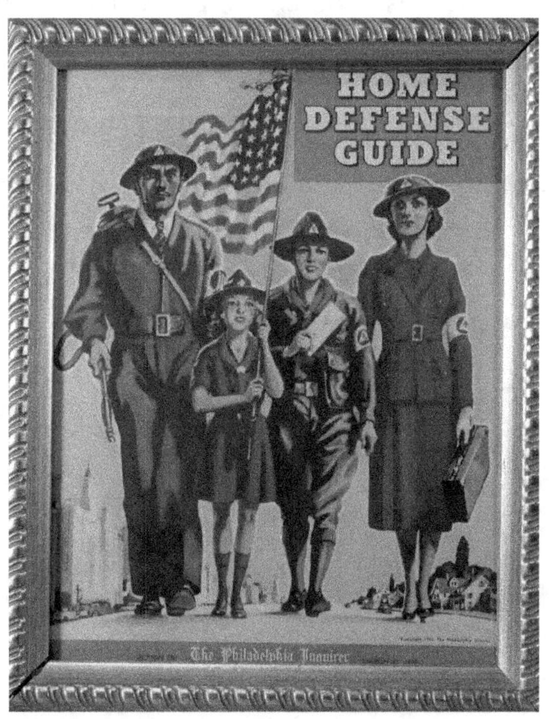

The Office of Civilian Defense was a United States federal emergency war agency set up in 1941 by Executive Order 8757. It coordinated state and federal measures for the protection of civilians in case of war emergencies. It supervised blackouts, fire protection, and special war services, including child care, housing, health and transportation.

The Civil Air Patrol and the Coast Guard Auxiliary used civilian spotters. All exterior lighting was extinguished, and black curtains covered windows. Fear of domestic attack in the United States encouraged Americans to accept a sacrifice economy. In 1942, a rationing program was established to control the amount of gas, food and clothing you could receive. Limits were set on the amount of gas, food and clothing consumers could purchase. Ration stamps were used to control supplies. Families used stamps to buy meat, sugar, fat, butter, gas, tires, clothing and fuel oil.

The United States Office of War Information released posters in which Americans were urged to "Do with less so they'll have enough." *They* referred to U.S. troops. Meanwhile, individuals and communities conducted drives for the collection of scrap, and purchased war bonds to pay for the war. A concept of *reuse* rather than *discard* or *recycling* was born, all to aid the war effort on as many economic fronts as possible. [47]

---

47   https://www.history.com/topics/world-war-ii/us-home-front-during-world-war-ii

HONOR FLAG

White minority participation in the U.S. Armed Forces during World War II 1

- Latino-American - 500,000

- Jewish-Americans - 550,000

- Polish-Americans - 1,000,000

- Italian-Americans - 1,500,000

- Arab-Americans - 30,000

- Armenian-Americans - 18,500   [48]

---

48   http://en.wikipedia.org/wiki/Ethnic_minorities_in_the_US_armed_forces_during_World_War_II

JOE LOUIS

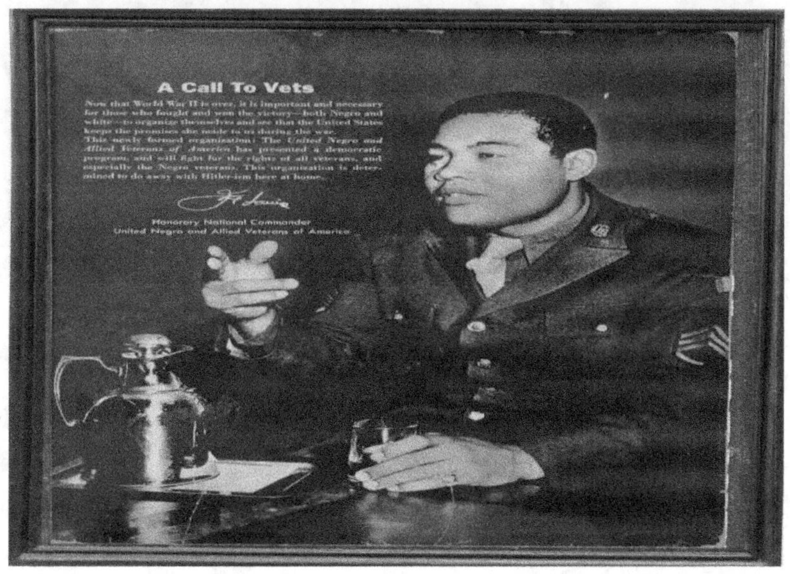

Joseph Louis Barrow (May 13, 1914 – April 12, 1981), known professionally as Joe Louis, was an American professional boxer who competed in the ring from 1934 to 1951. He reigned as the world heavyweight champion from 1937 to 1949 and is acknowledged to be one the greatest heavyweight boxers of all time. He enlisted in the Army during World War II and fought multiple promotional fights to improve military morale.

As a world champion, he used his status to champion desegregation during World War II, acting in the role of a "goodwill ambassador." Specifically, he fought to raise Army and Navy Relief funds. He refused to fight for segregated audiences. He helped in integrating

Army buses. He helped to prevent Jackie Robison's court martial, and he promoted enlistment and promotion in the service. He was a recipient of the Legion of Merit Award. [49]

____

49   https://www.sunsigns.org/famousbirthdays/d/profile/joe-louis/

MARCHING ON! & WHERE'S MY MAN TONITE? 1943 MOVIE

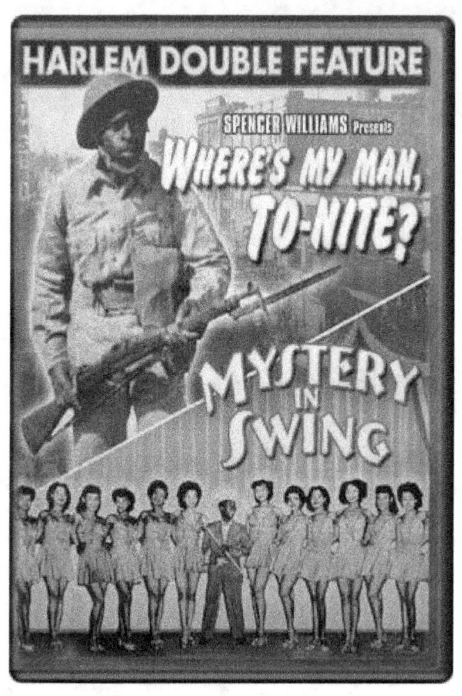

A thriving black independent film industry existed during the 1930s and 1940s. Marching On! was a 1943 black film. It follows a soldier in boot camp after being drafted into the Army during World War II. His family has a tradition of military service. The soldier becomes a hero when he locates the Japanese saboteurs operating a radio station outside the military base.

The film was written and directed by Spencer Williams. Sequences were filmed at Fort Huachuca, Arizona. The film was later rereleased with additional musical sequences under the title, *Where's My Man To-nite?* [50]

____

50   https://www.fesfilms.com/public-domain/black-heritage.html

FEMALE MILITARY TRENCH COAT

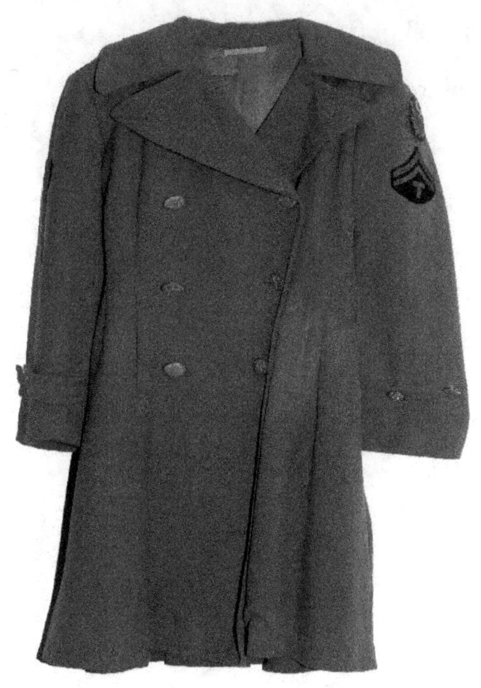

Wool coats offered great utility during the war. Warm in winter, cool in summer. Women served in the military during World War II. Women were in or near combat zones, especially nurses, but they did not have direct combat positions. Many used their nursing expertise for the war effort. There were Red Cross and military nurses. About 74,000 women served during World War II in the American Army and Navy Nurse Corps. Women also served in other military branches, often in traditional "women's work," secretarial duties or cleaning, for instance. Others freed men for combat by performing their duties.

Figures for women in each branch of the American military were:

- Army - 140,000
- Navy - 100,000
- Marines - 23,000
- Coast Guard - 13,000
- Air Force - 1,000
- Army and Navy Nurse Corps - 74,000

---

51   https://military.wikia.org/wiki/United_States_Army_uniforms_in_World War 2.

52   https://www.ibiblio.org/hyperwar/USA/ref/FM/index.html

DORIS MILLER

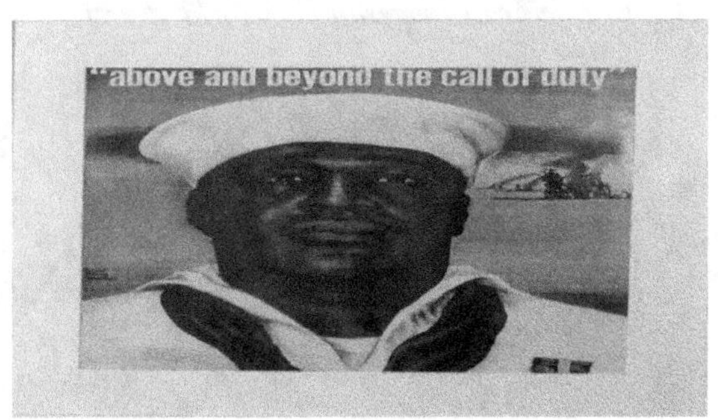

Doris Miller, known as "Dorie," was born in Waco, Texas, in 1919. After high school, he enlisted in the Navy as a mess attendant, or kitchen worker, to earn money for his family. At that time, the Navy was segregated, so combat positions were not open to African Americans. When the Japanese attacked Pearl Harbor on December 7, 1941, he immediately reported to his assigned battle station. Miller was quite athletic, so his job was to carry the injured to safer quarters. This included the mortally wounded ship's captain. Miller returned to the deck and saw that the Japanese planes were still dive-bombing the U.S. Naval Fleet. He picked up a 50-caliber Browning antiaircraft machine gun on which he had never been trained and managed to shoot down three to four enemy aircraft. He fired until he ran out of ammunition. He received the Navy Cross for his heroic act. Miller returned to service after selling war bonds. He was on a new ship that was torpedoed in 1944. [53]

---

53   americacomesalive.com/dorie-miller-1919-1943

AUDIE MURPHY

Most decorated veteran of World War II

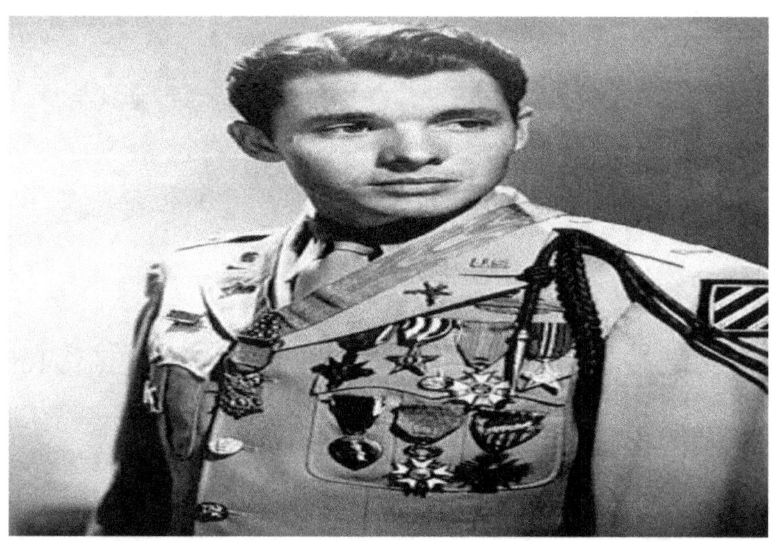

Audie Leon Murphy was an American soldier, actor, songwriter, rancher, and veterans' advocate. He was one of the most decorated soldiers of World War II. He received every military combat award available in the U.S. Army. He also received French and Belgian honors.

Audie Murphy suffered from Post-Traumatic Stress Disorder (PTSD), known in World War II as *Battle fatigue.* To help returning veterans, he spoke out about his problems, including difficulty with sleeping, not feeling safe and the need for mental health support. These were invisible wounds.

Invisible wounds like post-traumatic stress disorder, military sexual trauma, and other post-traumatic and exposure mental challenges are now recognized as possible consequences of military service. To help prevent veteran suicides, organizations like the ACES Veterans Museum and ACES Veterans Annex try to boost morale and provide referral services. The staff and Board of ACES Museum are also requested to undergo education at the federal program pschyarmor.org and others. [54] [55]

---

54   https://www.biography.com/military-figure/audie-murphy

55   http://www.americans-working-together.com/post_traumatic_stress_disorder_ptsd/id15.html#:~:text=Audie%20 Murphy%20sufferred%20from%

PAMELA "PAM" ARCHER MURPHY

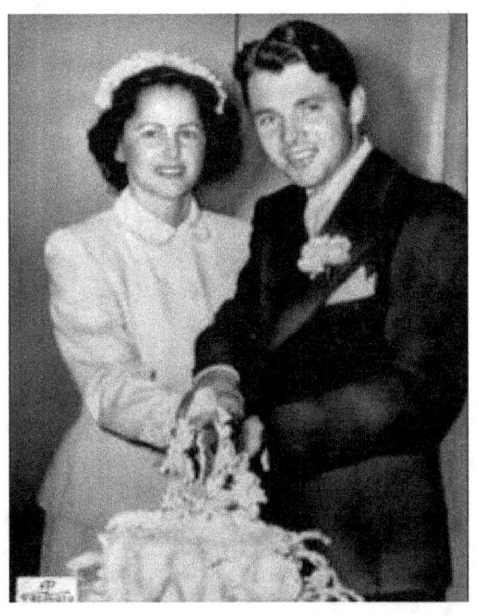

Pamela Murphy was the widow of Audie Murphy, the actor and wartime hero, but she had her own career serving Veterans full-time for 35 years at the Sepulveda Veteran's Administrative Hospital. She paid off her husband's debts and raised her sons in a modest apartment. Ms. Murphy was such an effective veterans' advocate that when budget cuts were proposed, they demanded she remained at the veterans hospital.

She was known to treat each veteran as a special person, scrupulously ensuring that all their needs were met. She considered each soldier or Marine to be a hero like her late husband.

Men with tears in their eyes would walk up to her in the hallway, and ask for a hug when they learned who she was. "Thank you," they said, over and over.

She was the one who held their hand when they were in pain, the one cutting through the red tape to get them to see the specialists they needed. She never looked for closing time to arrive. Rather, she only left when the last veteran on her clipboard had seen the doctor, and if one was still sitting there an hour after his appointment time, she thought nothing of taking him by the hand, and marching him past the objecting receptionist, and straight into the doctor's office.

Sadly, her husband, Audie Murphy, despite his distinguished wartime service, perhaps as a consequence of the PTSD of his veteran years, had died broke in a plane crash in 1971, after squandering millions of dollars on gambling, bad investments, and other women. *"Even with the adultery and desertion at the end, he always remained my hero,"* Pam later said of her husband. Pamela Murphy represents the devoted family members supporting the veterans, even in difficult circumstances. [56]

---

56   https://www.findagrave.com/memorial/51117433/pamela-opal_lee-murphy

DAISY MYERS

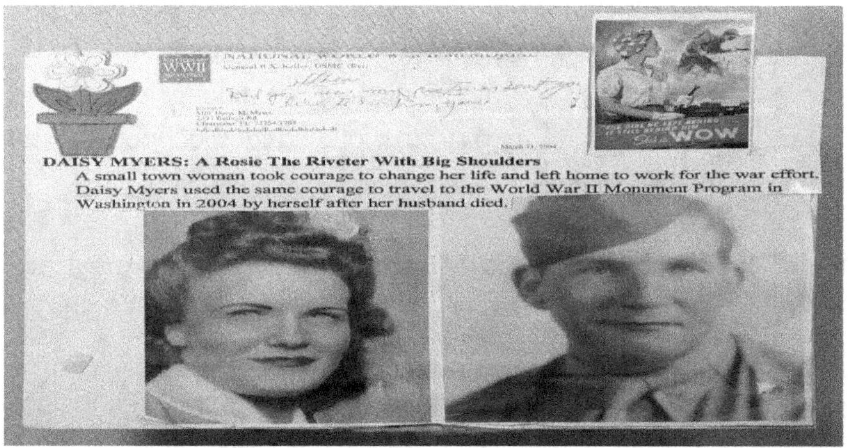

Rosie the Riveter was an allegorical cultural icon of World War II, and represented the women who worked in factories and shipyards during World War II. They produced munitions and war supplies. These women sometimes took entirely new jobs, replacing the male workers who joined the military. From 1941-1945, there were 20 million women added to the labor pool.

Daisy Myers was a *Rosie the Riveter* who met the author of this book, Dr. Althea Hankins, at the dedication of the World War II Memorial. Her husband had recently died, but she showed courage by supporting him and country, firstly, by leaving her "little town" to work in a factory while he was overseas during the war, and secondly, by coming to Washington DC to represent them both at the memorial. Dr. Hankins assured her that she would immortalize her late husband at ACES Museum in Philadelphia. There were 310,000 women, or 65% of the aircraft industry in 1943, compared to the 1% female employment rate prior to World War II. [57]

---

www.history.com/.../world-war-ii/rosie-the-riveter 57

NATIVE AMERICANS PATCH 1940

Native Americans in World War II

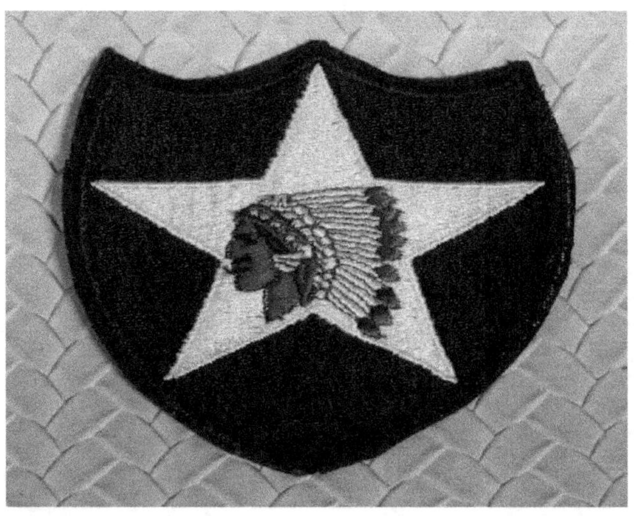

From 25,000 to 44,000 Native Americans fought actively in World War II. They were in intergraded units, in the Army, Navy, Marines, and Coast Guard. 800 Native American women served as nurses and joined the Women Army Corps (WACS). Over one-third of able-bodied Native American men aged 18 to 50 enlisted, making them the highest percentage ethnic group in the armed forces. The military population was as high as 70 percent of the population of some tribes. The strategy of using American Indians who were fluent in both their traditional tribal language and the English Language to send secret messages in battle was started in World War I. In World War II, there was a specific policy to recruit and train code talkers.

General Douglas MacArthur met with Navajo, O'odham, Pawnee and other native troops on December 31, 1943, to formalize the Code Talker Program. Navajo and other code talkers helped relay military secrets in the Pacific. To their credit, they managed to establish an unbreakable code. The program was removed from a secret status and formally awarded in 1982. [58] [59]

---

58   en.wikipedia.org/wiki/Native_Americans_and_World_War_II

59   www.intelligence.gov/.../453-navajo-code-talkers

NATIVE KINGS

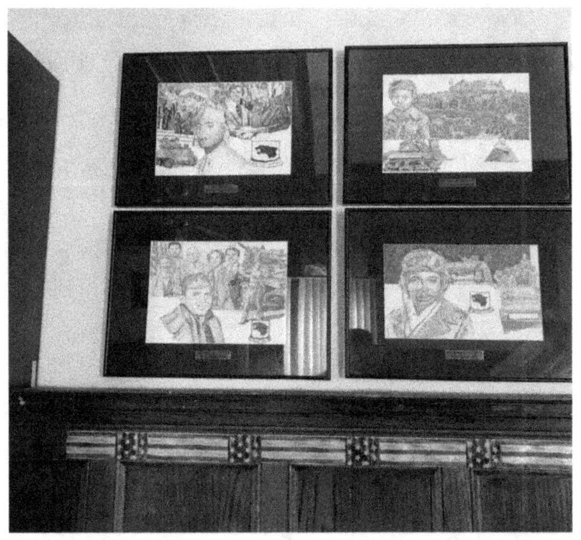

ACES Veterans Annex was discovered and created by Commander William "Bill" Maxey (Retired). ACES Veterans Annex was dedicated in 2019 as an enduring monument to the wartime efforts of the Black and minority veterans who served in World War II, and the love, respect, and support that their community accorded them.

ACES Annex was founded based on the template of the parent ACES Museum, and functions as a Veterans Service Organization (VSO). They also provide food and other services for the community at large. The staff also encourages veterans in all their undertakings and activities, and participates in the psycharmor. org education program.

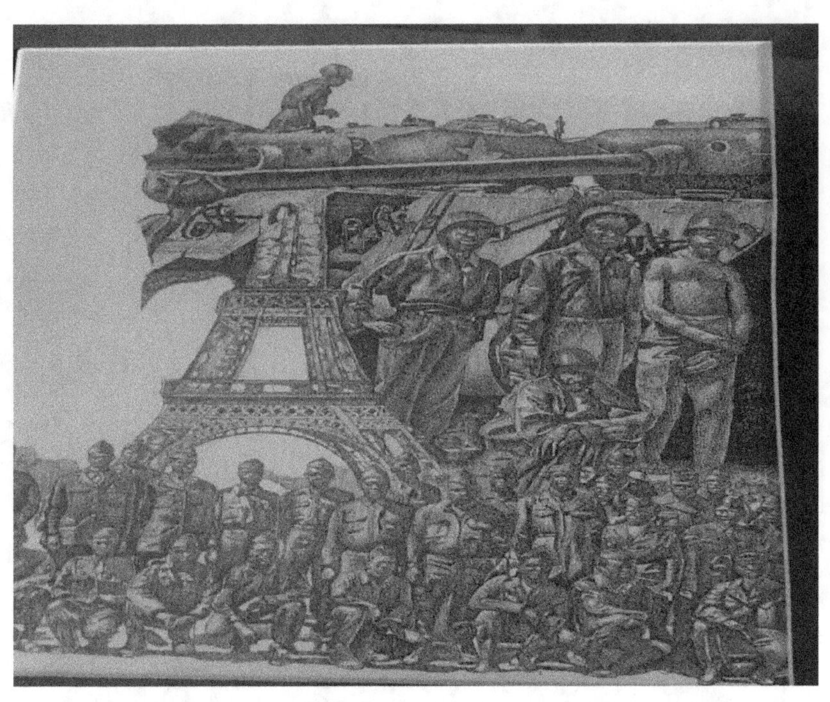

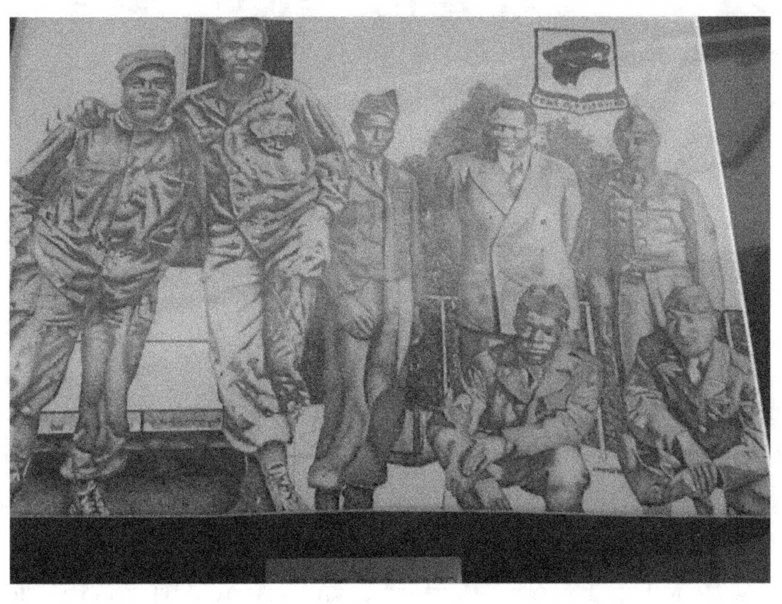

OAR

The Coast Guard

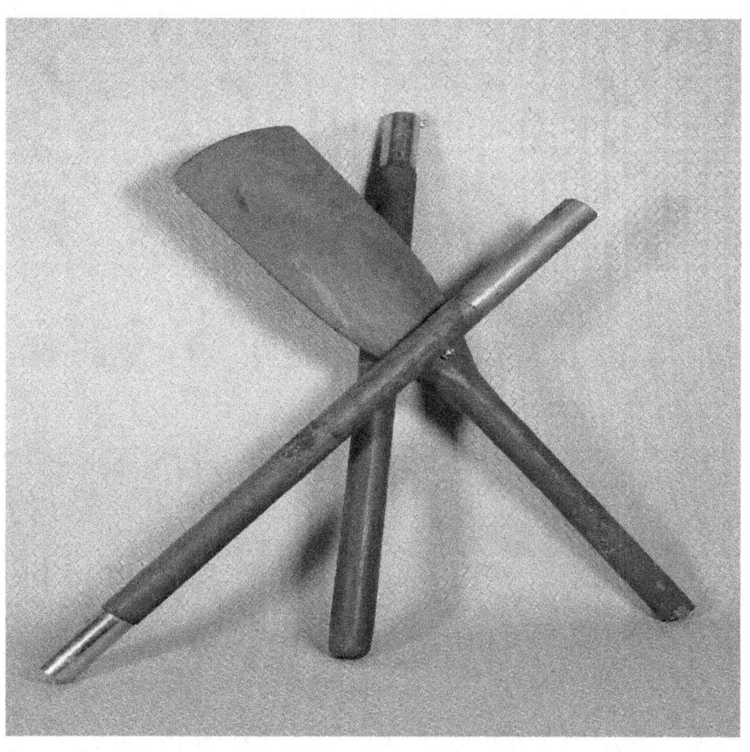

This official oar is representative of the wartime efforts of the Black people who served in the Coast Guard during World War II. In the 228 years of Coast Guard history, Blacks have been an integrated minority group that service branch. In the early years of the U.S. Revenue Cutter Service, many African American cutter men, both slaves and the free, served with white shipmates. In World War II, the Coast Guard undertook the federal government's first program in desegregation. African American Coast Guard candidates started in the Reserve Officer Training Program. In 1943, the Coast Guard began sending African American officer candidates through its Officer Training Program. 50 Black officers were assigned to the USS Sea Cloud and other sea vessels. By 1945 there were several black commanders.

In addition, five African American women enlisted in SPARS. The United States Coast Guard Reserve was known as SPARS. SPARS was started in 1942. Alex Haley, famous author of the book on the slave trade, "Roots," was a well-known journalist and Coast Guard member. He joined the Coast Guard in 1939 and retired 20 years later. Haley started the "Mail Call" article to address the need for mail services for the men. He was later promoted to enlisted journalist. For that promotion and support of the Coast Guard, Haley was honored by having a Cutter named for him, a special award named after him, and an honorary degree from the Coast Guard Academy. [60] [61] [62]

---

60   https://www.history.uscg.mil/Browse-by-Topic/Notable-People/Women/SPARS/

61   https://coastguard.dodlive.mil/2018/02/tlbl-african-americans-in-uscg-combat/

62   https://www.pacificarea.uscg.mil/Our-Organization/Cutters/cgcAlexHaley/

SEA BEES PAPERWEIGHT

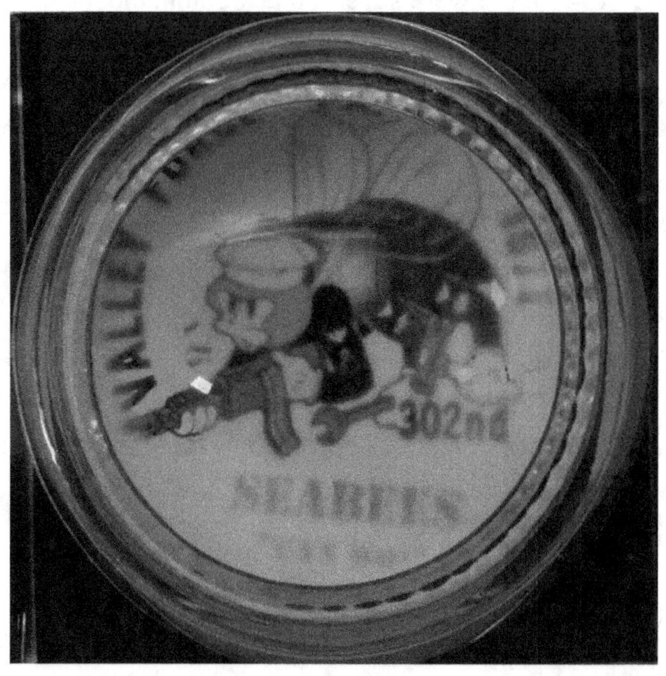

The Naval Construction Force, known as the *Seabees*, was created in 1942 to address the need for construction in combat zones during World War II. They were deployed around the world to provide engineering and construction services. African Americans were accepted into the Seabees. They endured Japanese bombing raids and five men were killed and 35 wounded in their first deployment. Their work in the Solomon Islands garnered numerous commendations and citations for exceptional service. In Trinidad, the 80th Naval Construction Battalion constructed a massive airship hangar and other airfield facilities in defense of the Caribbean Islands from German U-boat operations. First

Lady Eleanor Roosevelt and other dignitaries visited the unit to inspect their progress.

The Black members of the Battalion had to stage a hunger strike in 1945 because of unfair duty schedules and delay or lack of promotions. Thurgood Marshall and the NAACP were also involved in securing basic rights in the Navy Seabees. The Southern officers were replaced with fair-complexioned officers in a clear case of racial prejudice. The U.S. Navy Seabee Museum is a plaque from World War II that states "Proving Our Worth" for the 20th NSBs. It was a description of men fighting against fascism and racism. More than 12,500 African American men served in the Seabees in the Atlantic and the Pacific. In 1944, the Pacific units were integrated. By late 1945 the black and white Seabees were the Navy's first fully integrated units. [63]

____

63   https://www.history.navy.mil/browse-by-topic/communities/seabees1.html

PARATROOPERS SUPPORT POSTER 19240

Triple Nickels

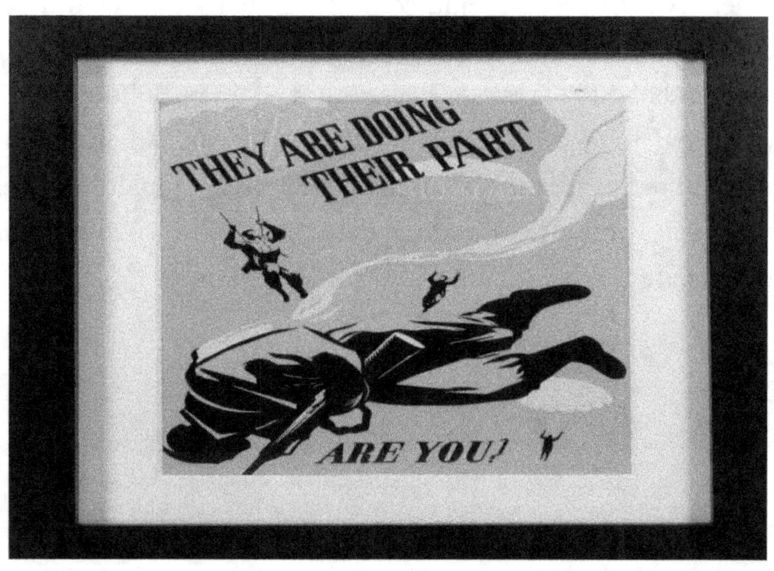

The Triple Nickels was the nickname of the 555th Parachute Infantry Battalion, the nation's first Black paratrooper unit. The Battalion would later be folded into the 82nd Airborne Division. They were composed of "exceptional men, college-educated, and professional athletes." It existed from 1944-1947. The 555th would refine many special operations that are still in use today.

The 555th was involved in a secret mission to tackle Japanese military incursion on American soil in the winter of 1944-45. 9,300 Fu-Go balloon bombs were sent and 1000 actually reached America territory. The Triple Nickels had to find, detonate and remove these bombs. They also had to extinguish associated fires that resulted from the explosives. The 555th worked on twenty-eight fires in 1945. The paratroopers actually jumped into 15 of these fires. They lost one trooper. The 555th was part of the "colored test platoon" from the 92nd Infantry (Buffalo) Division.[64]

----

64 https://www.opb.org/news/article/triple-nickles-pendleton-oregon-history-smokejumpers/

PARKER HALL ACES MUSEUM

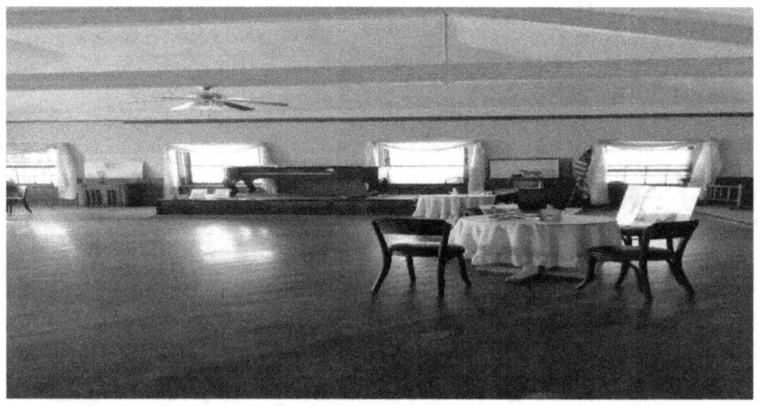

Parker Hall was certified as a functioning USO for Black soldiers in World War II by the Germantown Historic Society in Philadelphia, Pennsylvania. Due to segregation in the 1940s, Blacks had to set up independent support systems. Parker Hall was one of such places. Although Parker Hall was a Black facility, the decision was made by ACES founders to create a museum that would reflect minority stories that were often omitted from World War II narratives and history in general. ACES Veterans Museum has been dedicated to the preservation of Parker Hall and the history of Black and minority Veterans of World War II and their families. Programs have consistently run at the Parker Hall museum since 2001.

ACES Museum was certified as a Veteran Support Organization (VSO) by the City of Philadelphia in 2009 to facilitate its help referral network. Staff members are encouraged to get training by psycharmor.org. This federal program encourages education to assist in improving Veteran's support. In 2016, ACES Museum was awarded the 800-pound Vietnam Memorial Plaque for her commitment to Vietnam Veterans. Motto: *"Every Day Is Veterans Day at ACES."*

The items in the book are from ACES Veterans Museum Annex, Pontiac, with the intention of preserving the Native King's paintings and the history of Black and minority Veterans in Pontiac, Michigan. [65]

---

65   For further information: acesmuseum.online. and aces museum You Tube videos. https://psycharmor.org/

GENERAL PATTON MEDAL

National Archives and Parker Hall

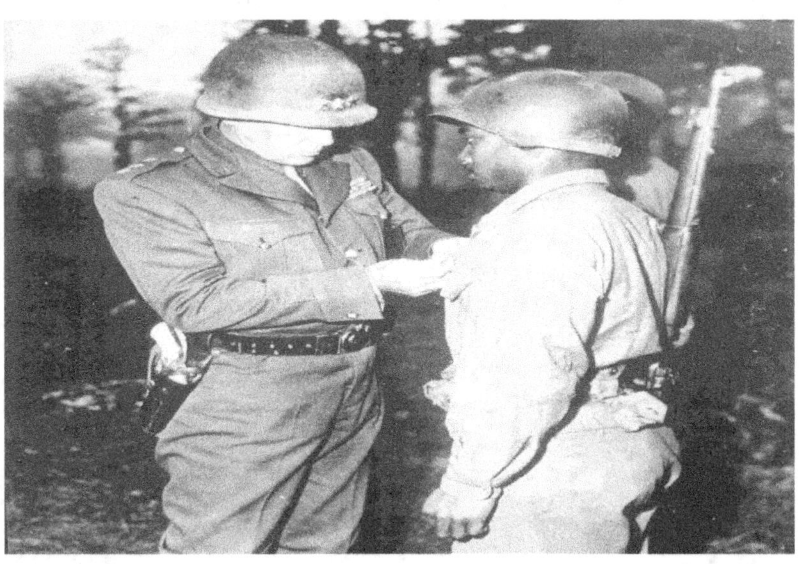

General George S. Patton, U.S. Third Army commander, pinning the Silver Star on Private Ernest A. Jenkins of New York City after the liberation of France, 1944. In 1944, the all-black 761st Tank Battalion became the first African American unit assigned to General George S. Patton's Third Army in France. Patton said, *"You're the first Negro tankers to ever fight in the American Army. I would never have asked for you if you weren't good. I have nothing but the best in my Army. I don't care what color you are as long as you go up there and kill*

those Kraut sons of bitches. Everyone has their eyes on you and is expecting great things from you. Don't let them down and damn you, don't let me down!" [66]

----

66   history.com/news/761st-tank-battalion-black-panthers-liberators-battle-of-the-bulgue

PLASTER

Nisei Troops

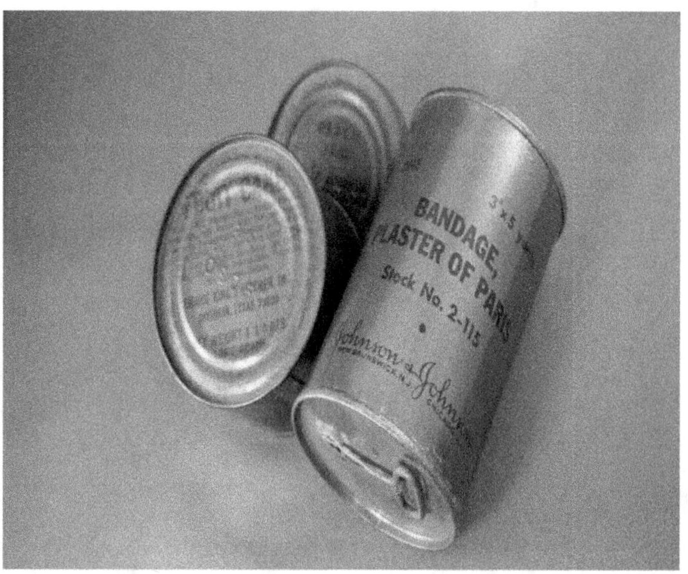

The Nisei were second-generation Japanese who served in the military while their families were placed in camps because of racist fears emanating from the provisions of Executive Order 9066. Issued by President Franklin Roosevelt on February 19, 1942, this order authorized the forced removal of all persons deemed a threat to national security from the West Coast to "relocation centers" further inland, resulting in the incarceration of Japanese Americans.

Between 1861 and 1940, approximately 275,000 Japanese immigrated to Hawaii and the mainland United States, the majority arriving between 1898 and 1924, when quotas were adopted that ended Asian immigration. On December 7, 1941, the Empire of Japan attacked the United States at the Pearl Harbor Naval Base in Hawaii. The attack launched a rash of fear about national security, especially on the West Coast. This combined with economic competition, distrust over cultural separateness, and long-standing anti-Asian racism turned into disaster for Japanese Americans.

Lobbyists from western states, many representing competing economic interests or nativist groups, pressured Congress and the President to remove persons of Japanese descent from the west coast, both foreign born (issei – meaning "first generation" of Japanese in the U.S.) and American citizens (nisei – the second generation of Japanese in America, U.S. citizens by birthright).

While German prisoners of war were freely going to the movies, the Japanese lost their homes, businesses, and freedom. When allowed to serve, 33,000 Japanese Americans entered the service. 20,000 joined the Army. The segregated Nisei troops, the 100th Infantry Battalion, were composed of men from Hawaii. They entered combat in Italy and suffered such horrific casualties that they became known as the *Purple Heart Battalion*. The 1st Battalion of the 442nd had to send replacement troops to join the 100th in early 1944. The 2nd and 3rd Battalions shipped out on May 1, 1944, joining the 100th in Italy in June 1944. For its size and length of service, the Nisei unit was the most decorated in U.S. military history.

The Japanese were sent for Allied Language Training and worked in non-combat roles translating enemy documents and interrogating prisoners of war. They helped translate 18,000 enemy documents, created 16,000 propaganda leaflets and interrogated over 10,000 Japanese POWs. As servicemen, they were present at every major battle against Japanese forces. They sometimes suffered under friendly fire from U.S. soldiers, unable to distinguish them from the Japanese troops. Japanese American women volunteered for the service when they were allowed. [67]

____

67 https://en.wikipedia.org/wiki/Japanese_American_service_in_World_War_II#Servicemen_in_the_Army_Air_Forces

PUERTO RICAN PLATE

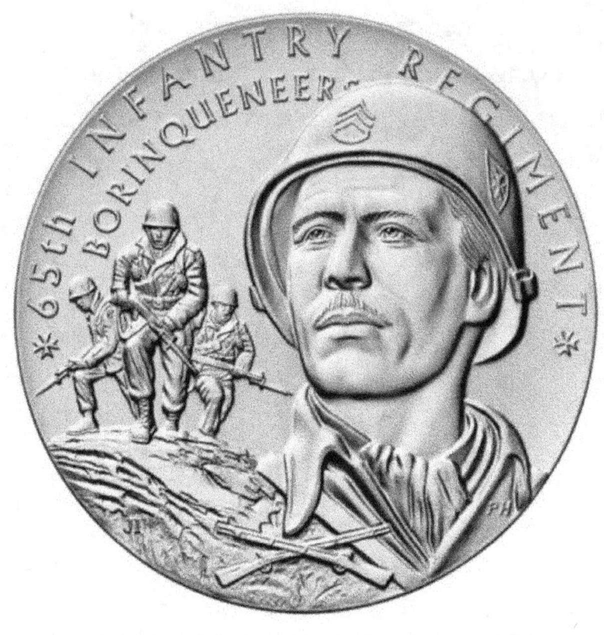

Puerto Ricans were treated as two separate groups during World War II. The *white* Puerto Ricans were the 65th Infantry, a segregated unit for whites only. They were also in the National Guard. The black Puerto Ricans served in black units, including the 99th Fighter Squadron and the Tuskeegee Airmen. They served in all branches of the armed forces, including the Harlem Hell Fighters, which was formed in New York. The 369th Infantry Regiment, formerly known as the 15th New York National Guard Regiment, was commonly referred to as the Harlem Hellfighters. This was a New York Army National Guard infantry regiment during World War I and World War II. The Regiment consisted mainly of African Americans but also included several Puerto Rican Americans during World War II. With the 370th Infantry Regiment, it was known for being one of the first African American regiments to serve with the American troops.

Hispanic Americans, also referred to as Latinos, served in all elements of the American armed forces in the war. They were involved in every major American battle in the war. Between 400,000 and 500,000 Hispanic Americans served in the U.S. Armed Forces during World War II, out of a total of 16,000,000, constituting 3.1% to 3.2% of the U.S. Armed Forces.

Over 200 Puerto Rican women served in nursing and administration during World War II. Carmen Contreras Boaz was the first Hispanic WAC. She served in the Army from 1941-1945 and formed a chapter of WAC Veterans and the Society of Military Widows. The military did not keep statistics regarding the total number of Hispanics who served in the regular Armed Forces units, but only those who served in Puerto Rican units. Therefore, it is impossible to determine the exact number of Puerto Ricans who served in World War II. [68] [69] [70]

68   en.wikipedia.org/wiki/Hispanic_Americans_in...

69   https://www.history.com/this-day-in-history/puerto-ricans-become-u-s-citizens-are-recruited-for-war-effort

70   https://www.liquisearch.com/puerto_ricans_in_world_war_ii

PURPLE HEART AND MEDALS

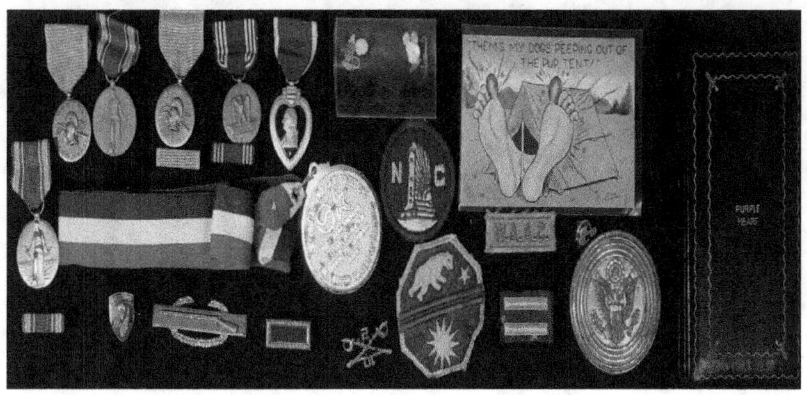

There were multiple black Field Artillery Units in World War II. The 46th Field Artillery Brigade was the largest brigade formed of black troops in 1941. They were battery operators, telegraphy experts, and code specialists and had a band, orchestra, and diverse training areas. The 350 Field Artillery Regiment was a black unit specializing in switchboards, trucks, and medical and dental sections.

Other notable African American units that served in World War II were:

- 92nd Infantry Division
- Marine Units (2)
- 93rd Infantry Division
- Army Nurses

- 2nd Cavalry Division
- WACS Army
- Air Corps Unit 332d Fighter Group
- WAVES Navy
- Field Artillery Units (32)
- SPARS Coast Guard
- 452nd Anti-Aircraft Artillery Battalion
- Navy Nurses
- 555th Parachute Infantry Battalion
- U.S. Military Academy Cavalry Squadron
- 5th Reconnaissance Squadron
- Tank Battalions (3)
- Tank Destroyer Units (11)

---

71   https://digicom.bpl.lib.me.us/cgi/viewcontent.
cgi?article=1063&context=ww_reg_his

72   https://www.liquisearch.com/military_history_of_african_americans/world_
war_ii/units

73   https://guides.loc.gov/african-american-women-military/books

WORLD WAR II SABOTAGE WANTED POSTER

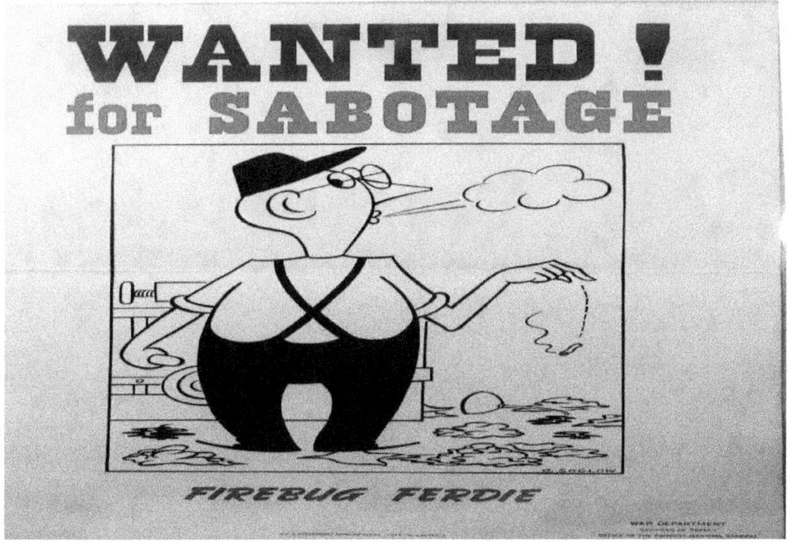

Sabotage, in the overseas frontlines, primarily involved the Resistance derailing trains. In the United States, the fire, destruction, and possible sabotage, of the Normandie Ship in New York led the Navy to address sabotage on water. They formed a partnership with Charles "Lucky" Luciano, the Italian-born gangster and mafia boss, to prevent further sabotage on the docks by Germans who had massively infiltrated the country.

Although Luciano was in jail for mafia-related crimes, he was still able to exert control over the docks. He did not want to live in a country that was ruled by the dictator Mussolini and, instructed his "capos" to act as lookouts for German activities. He also assisted in the United States' and the Allies' invasion of Sicily in 1943. He provided maps and local contacts for aid. There was not another boat fire during World War II at the docks. Luciano was pardoned after the war in 1946 and then deported to his homeland of Italy. [74]

---

74   https://www.historynet.com/the-fate-of-the-ss-normandie.htm

SNUFF BOXES

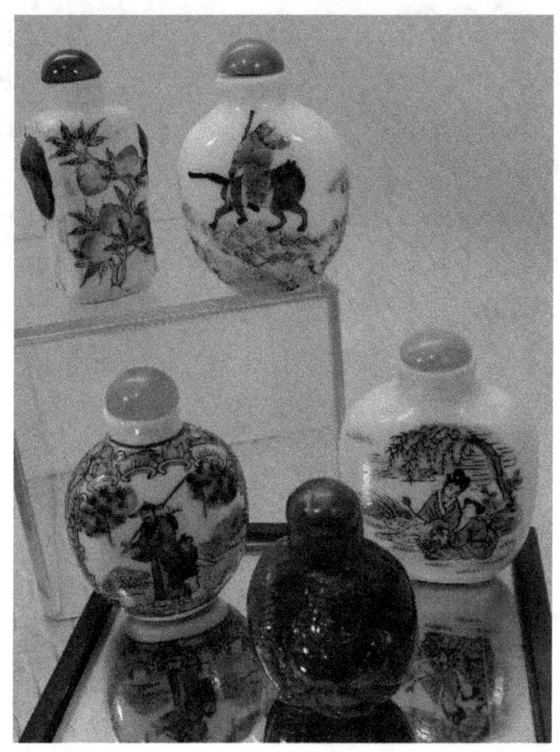

Snuffbox is a small ornamented box for holding snuff (scented, powdered tobacco). The practice of sniffing or inhaling a pinch of snuff was common in England around the 17th century. When, in the 18th century, it became widespread in other countries as well, the demand for decorated snuffboxes, considered valuable gifts, increased.

Snuff boxes were used to house powdered tobacco. They were more popular than smoking in the 18th and 19th centuries. World

War II made it hard to acquire them from overseas. They were later replaced with cigarettes which was a more glamorous way to inhale tobacco.

The effects of snuff and smoking were not exposed until cigarette,warning labels were placed on packages in 1969. Vaping is the new glamorous way of processing toxic tobacco through e-cigarettes and e-juice. The vape machine heats up the juice and it is inhaled. Vaping is associated with cardiovascular disease, increased bacteria and gum disease, and decreased brain development for those under 25 years of age. Time studies indicate it will eventually be associated with cancer like other tobacco products. [75] [76]

---

75 www.britannica.com/art/snuffbox

76 https://blog.vapefuse.com/11-things-you-need-to-know-about-vaping-tobacco/#:~:text=Side%20Effects%20of%20Smoking%20Tobacco%3A%20 1%20Lung%2C%20Heart,chemica

DICE AND CARDS

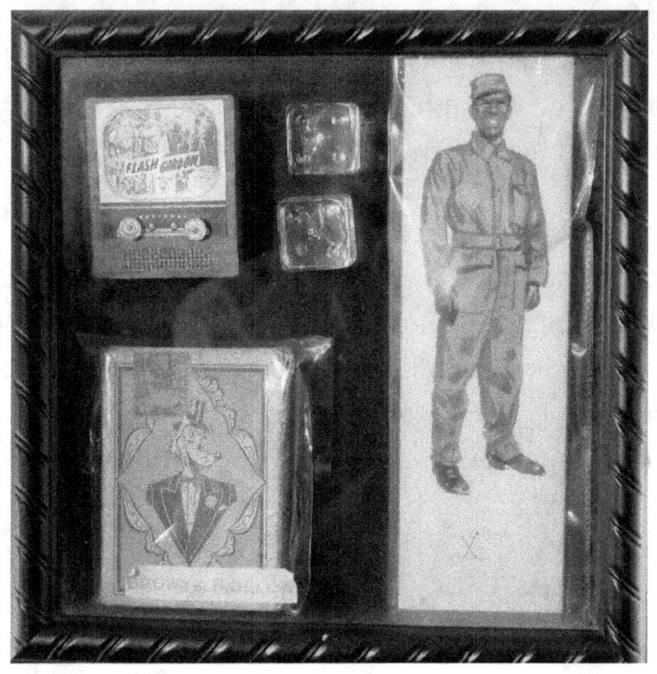

Playing cards were introduced to Europe in the 12th century by Arabs. They had been in Asia and Africa in the 9th Century. Some scholars think that playing cards were invented in China during the Tang dynasty around the 9th century A.D. and that they used woodblock, thereby promoting technology. Dice are the oldest gaming implements known to man. The Greek Sophocles (496 - 406 BC), a poet, claimed that the Greek Palamedes, during the siege of Troy, invented dice.

World War II veterans have had tremendous influence on the world of science fiction. Two of the major influencers of science fiction predicted items that would be produced in the future, and characters that would fight against tyranny. They were Marine Alexander Raymond and Army Air Force member Gene Roddenberry.

Alexander Gillespie Raymond Jr. was an American cartoonist best known for creating the *Flash Gordon* comic strip in 1934. Flash Gordon was a hero who battled space monsters, power-mad alien dictators and other threats to the stability of the universe.

Raymond joined the war effort first by having Flash Gordon fight dictators in 1941 in the comics. In 1944 he joined the war in earnest as a captain in the Marines. He created a patch for VMT B-143 that dubbed them the "Rocket Raiders." Raymond would continue to support the Marines by making his next comic book hero, Rib Kirby, a Marine reservist who worked as a detective for justice. Gene Roddenberry, an Army Air Force World War II Veteran and policeman, believed in scientific exploration, military might to protect and serve liberty, and human diversity as an asset and not something to be feared. The commitment to justice and improved racial relationswould cost him a television show. While writing *The Lieutenant,* he was refused support on an episode because he wanted to feature both black and white Marines.

Roddenberry's optimism, and his belief that different nationalities, races and species can happily create a better future, was the basis for *Star Trek*. The original show had respect for the unknown, and that the future could be wonderful, not something gloomy with assets restricted to the powerful few. His idealist response to the racial division of the sixties made him a Japanese helmsman, combating racism during World War II. He also installed a beautiful black female scientist who played a role as a model to millions in linguistics, cryptography and philology.

A half-Vulcan was to symbolize prejudice and the struggle for emotional control. Roddenberry was to pay a financial price for his convictions. Star Trek was canceled, and he had difficulty meeting financial obligations. Something rather unique then happened. The Star Trek universe and the concept of racial harmony and a fair and pleasant future refused to go away. It became "the show that wouldn't die." Trekkers and other fans would support him and Star Trek, creating their own movies and books. They believed you should "live long and prosper." Multiple Star Trek movies, books, and television shows have been created. There are currently three Star Trek television shows, with two others pending.

The casting of Nichols was groundbreaking. It was a rarity to see a black woman on primetime TV. It was even rarer to see a woman cast in a high-powered role.' Nichelle Nichols portrayal of Lieutenant Uhura in the sci-fi series was light years ahead of its time. She had the first interracial kiss in an American TV series. She worked with NASA and civil rights leaders who hailed her as a role model to millions. When she was going to quit, Dr. Martin Luther King asked her to stay and remain a positive example. She did. When Dr. Hankins, author of this book, met her at a Star Trek convention, she thanked Ms. Nichols for remaining a light for others to follow. Ms. Nichols said she was proud of her.

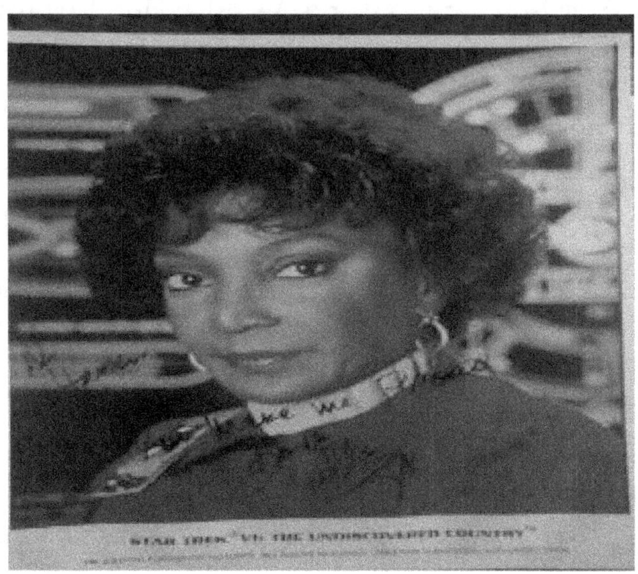

77   https://playingcarddecks.com/blogs/all-in/history-playing-cards-modern-deck

78   www.dice-play.com/History.htm

79   https://search.yahoo.com/search?fr=mcafee&type=C211US105D20151123&p=alex+raymond+flash+gordon

80   https://en.wikipedia.org/wiki/Gene_Roddenberry

81   https://www.theguardian.com/tv-and-radio/2016/oct/18/star-trek-nichelle-nichols-martin-luther-king-trekker

GEORGE AND JANICE TAYLOR

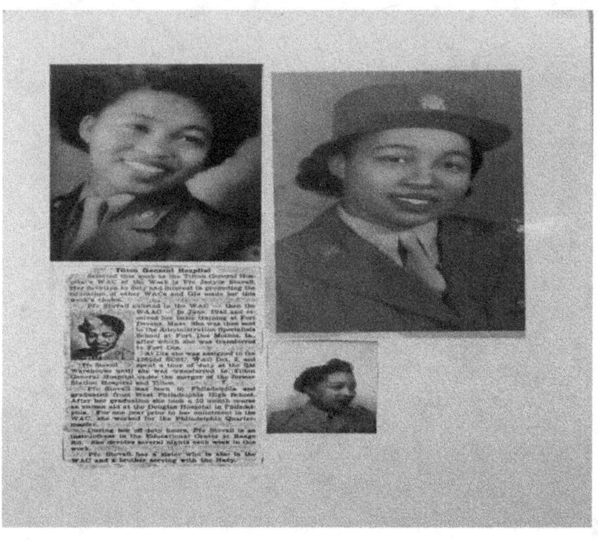

George Taylor was a World War II veteran who served in the Army in World War II, and in the Air force in Korea. Janice Taylor was in the 6888th, only black WAC unit to serve overseas in World War II. The 6888th Central Postal Directory Battalion was nicknamed the *"Six Triple Eight."* It was composed of black women, both enlisted and officers. The unit was led by Major Charity Adams Earley. They were given the impossible task of sorting and delivering one million pieces of discarded mail. Nevertheless, they completed the task earlier than expected in 1945. George and Janice Taylor were the founding fathers of the ACES Museum. [82]

---

82   https://en.wikipedia.org/wiki/6888th_Central_Postal_Directory_Battalion

THE FORGOTTEN FIRST

B-1 and The Integration of The Modern Navy

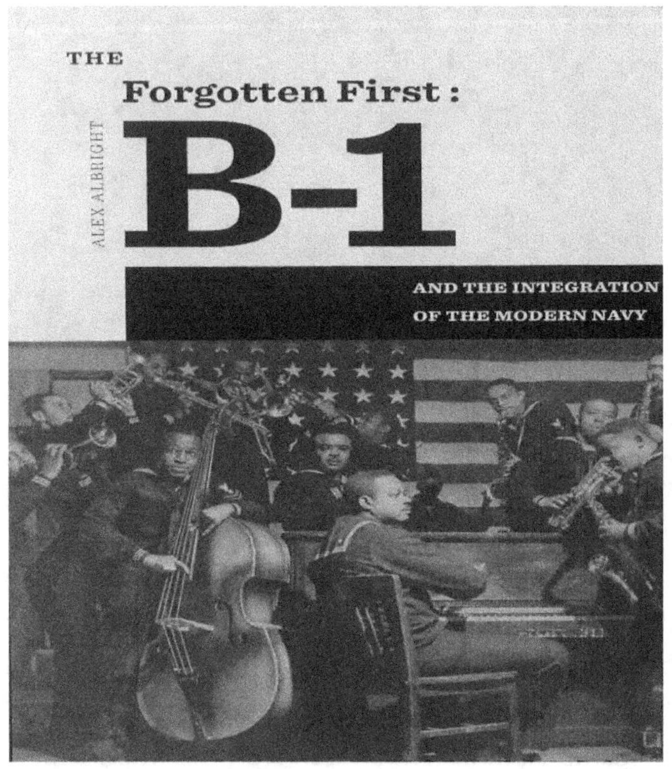

This book tells the history of one of the Navy's two all-black pre-flight training school bands. They volunteered and used music to foster integration, build morale, and re-enforce that blacks could function as sailors in full capacity. The volunteers were representing the reintegration of the Navy. In the nineteenth century, the Navy had only between was 20 and 30 Blacks, but this number had fallen to ½ of 1 percent by 1920.

Black leaders called for desegregation and a *Double Victory Campaign* in the United States during World War II. In 1941 President Roosevelt responded by placing 5,000 black bands on battleships to help racial relations. The President also called for 5,000 blacks to be recruited to serve on small harbor craft and at naval shore establishments in the Caribbean. In 1943, there were 26,909 black sailors. In 1944, the first commissioned black officers were received in the Navy. They were known as the *Golden Thirteen*. [83] [84] [85]

83   https://www.questia.com/library/journal/1G1-414272412/the-forgotten-first-b-l-and-the-integration-of-the#:~:text=Alex%20Albright%27s%20The%20 Forgotten

84   https://www.history.navy.mil/browse-by-topic/wars-conflicts-and-operations/world-war-ii/1942/manning-the-us-navy/african-americans-in-general-service--1942.html

85   https://www.britannica.com/topic/Golden-Thirteen

THE WHITE ROSE

The White Rose (weisserose) is named after a Spanish novel, *Rosa Blanco*. The White Rose was a group of students and professors who supported Civil Rights and opposed Nazi policies during World war II. They urged students to think for themselves about the atrocities that were being carried out in their name. The group's name and symbol were either named for a book or the white rose, meaning purity. Free thought is pure.

In the summer of 1942, several members that would form the White Rose served three months on the Russian front. They saw the horrors of war and the mistreatment of Jews. They returned home with the thought there was a moral obligation to act on one's beliefs. The White Rose produced literature that challenged state brutality. The goal was to arouse the public sentiment and compassion. The hopes of the White Rose members that German opposition would be active against the Nazi regime and the war effort did not come to pass on a massive scale. On the contrary, Nazi propaganda called on the German people to embrace "Total War" and ethnic purity.

"Why do you allow these men who are in power to rob you step by step, openly and in secret, of one domain of your rights after another, until one day nothing, nothing at all will be left but a mechanized state system presided over by criminals and drunks? Is your spirit already so crushed by abuse that you forget it is your right—or rather, your moral duty—to eliminate this system?" - 3rd leaflet of the White Rose. [86]

---

86   www.thoughtco.com/world-war-ii-the-white-rose-2361252#:~:text=The%20
White%20Rose%20

POSTER RECREATION

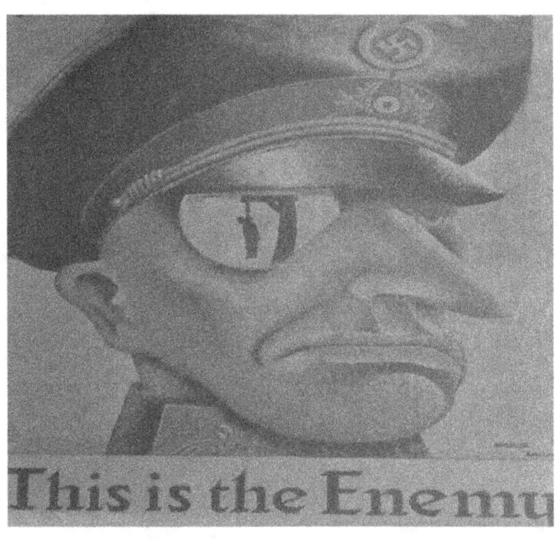

World War II propaganda was distributed in a variety of ways. There were leaflets, radio, television, and most importantly, the Poster. Posters were designed to be creative, colorful, eye-catching, and stimulate thought and support. There were over 200,000 posters designed and printed during World War II. They covered a variety of subject matters, and included things related to the war effort, such as wartime manufacturing, health and safety issues, war bonds, military recruitment, and, as already noted, racism and its effect on the war's positive production. The posters were created by federal agencies, commissions, and councils, as well as non-federal organizations. [87]

---

87 www.bartleby.com/essay/Propaganda-During-World-War-Two-FKJFNRFZTC

TILTED HAT VETERAN
SAM HILL

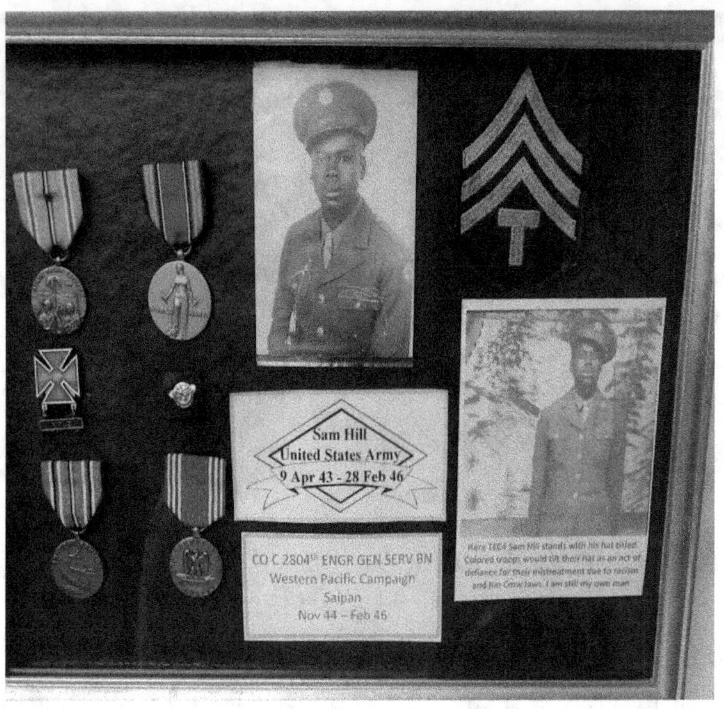

Sam Hill was a part of the black soldiers that served proudly and effectively in the Pacific. The medals testify to his patriotic conduct during a difficult set of circumstances. Yet, he still tilted his hat, acknowledging that he was his own man despite Jim Crow laws. Major Deborah Gary USAF, his daughter, is on the Advisory Board of ACES Veterans Museum.

TOURNIQUET

Dr. Charles Drew

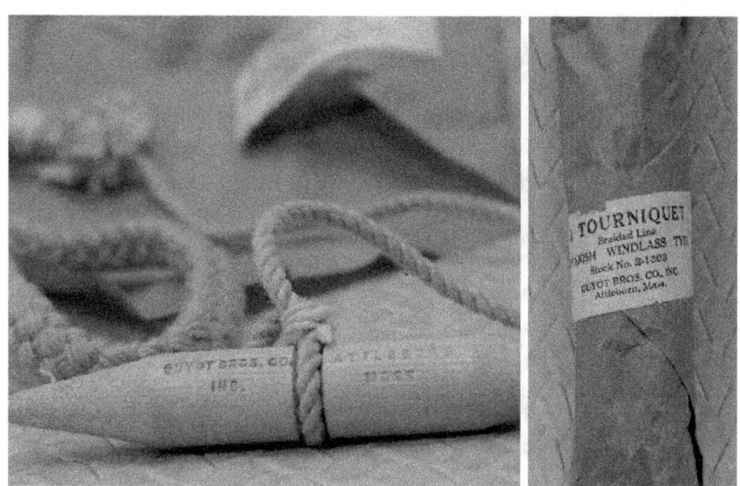

Dr. Charles Richard Drew, an African American physician, developed ways to process and store blood plasma. He preserved this blood plasma without cells so it would last longer and be reconstituted. He directed blood banks in the United States and Britain but resigned from the United States because the Red Cross would only give black blood to blacks, denying them access to most of the processed blood.

During World War II, most of the blood taken for use was processed into plasma. The plasma was shipped directly to the Army and Navy. This plasma was credited by the surgeons-general of the Army and Navy as being the greatest lifesaver of World War II. Plasma was even viewed as more important in preventing death during World War II than the new antibiotic penicillin. Plasma allowed more detailed and large scale directed surgeries, saving lives and limbs.

Dr. Drew's dried plasma became a vital element in the treatment of wounded soldiers during World War II. The Red Cross ended its World War II blood program for the military in World War II after collecting more than 13 million pints. [88] [89] [90]

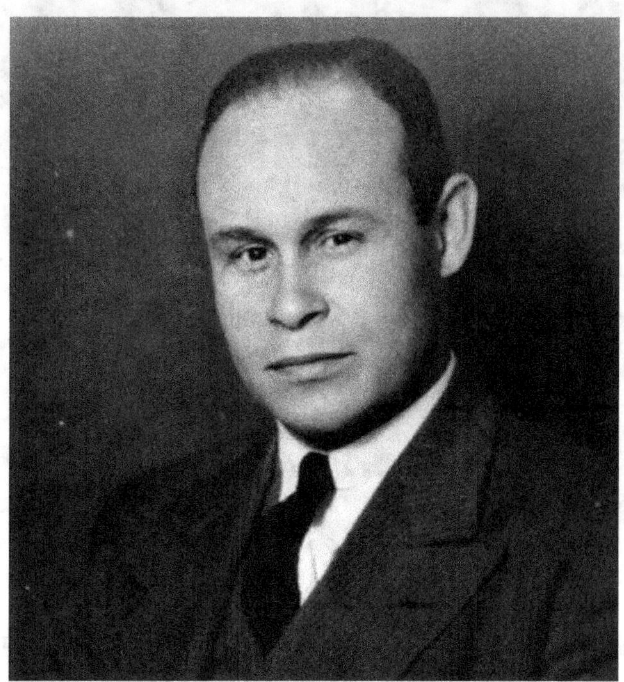

---

88   https://www.biography.com/scientist/charles-drew

89   https://www.britannica.com/science/history-of-medicine/World-War-II-and-after

90   www.britannica.com/.../World-War-II-and-after

TOY TRAINS - 1940S

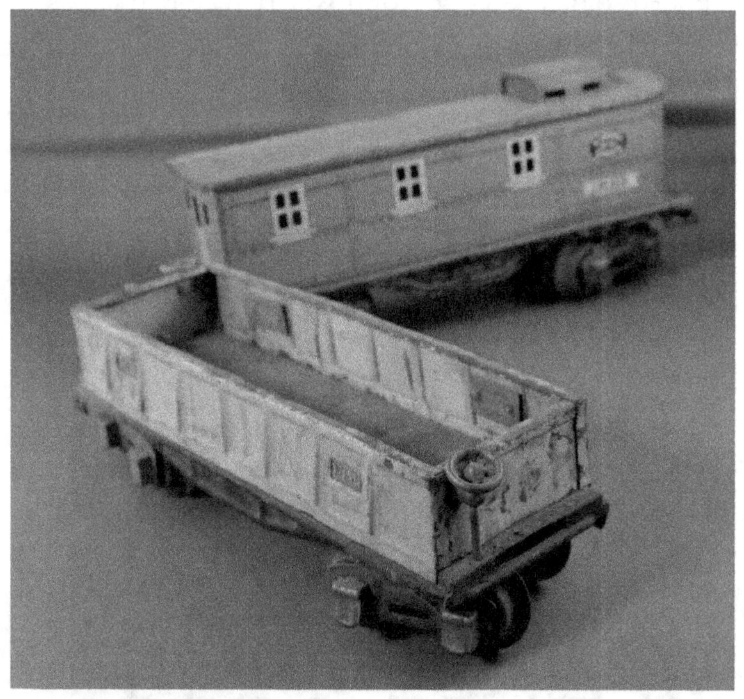

Trains were very popular during and after World War II. These trains had a tremendous recreational impact on children during World War II.

TUSKEGEE AIRPLANE

Official Tuskegee Model Airplane 1940s

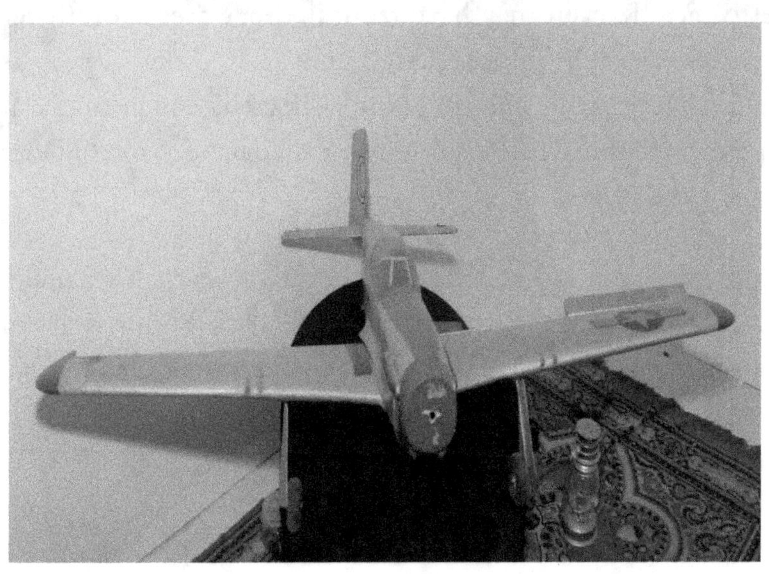

Herbert and Mildred Carter were married for nearly 70 years and were known as Tuskegee's "First Couple." Herbert Carter was one of the original Tuskegee Airmen pilots of the nation's first military program for black flyers. He earned his wings as a Second Lieutenant in 1942 and the rank of Lieutenant Colonel in a 27-year Air Force career. He was also ranked as a fighter pilot and squadron maintenance chief. The Tuskegee airmen would never stray from the bombers they protected. Therefore, only a handful of the planes they escorted were lost. They painted their planes as red tails.

Mildred Hemmons Carter entered college at 15. She learned to fly under C. Alfred "Chief" Anderson, the father of Black aviation. She became the first black woman in the state to earn her pilot's license while at Tuskegee. The First Lady, Ms. Roosevelt, visited that day. In 1941, Mildred became the first female pilot to join the state's Civil Air Patrol Squadron. In 1942 she applied to become a Women Air Force Service Pilot (WASP), but was turned down due to race. Racism may have truncated her dream of flying in the military, but she piloted planes until 1965. After 70 years, she received a letter from the government that she had been declared a member of the WASPs and given a medal, *The First Women in History to Fly America."*

The Carter's home became an aviation museum with multiple awards from several sources. The biggest honor was their enduring love. The "I believe I can Fly" *Puppets with History* show highlights Tuskegee airmen and women. [91]

---

91   www.cnn.com/2012/01/22/us/tuskegee-airmen-first-couple

VICTORY AND PEACE PAMPHLET

Victory Gardens. George Washington Carver

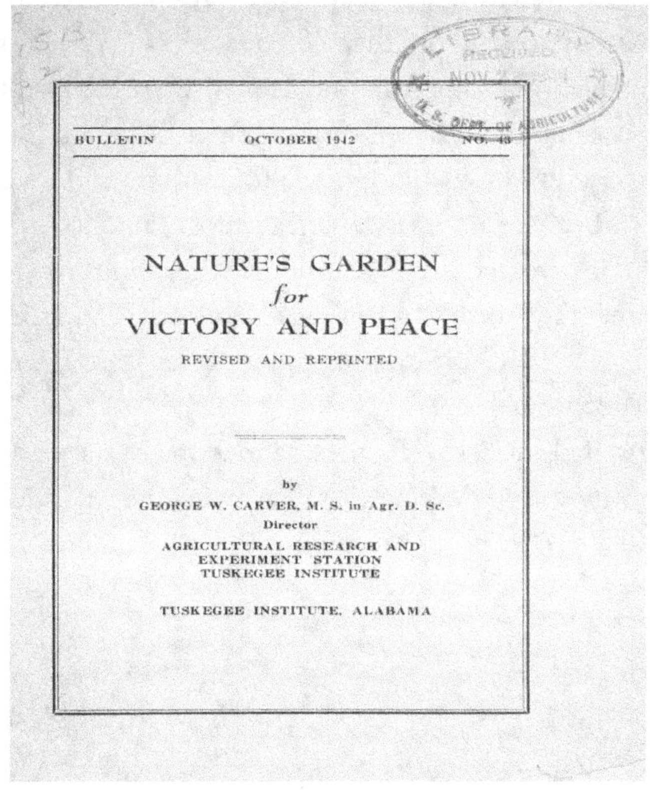

Victory gardens were encouraged during World War II. Commercial crops were diverted to the military overseas and the introduction of food rationing in the United States started in 1942. Americans had an incentive to grow their own fruits and vegetables in whatever locations they could find, including small flower boxes, apartment rooftops, backyards or deserted lots of any size. Eleanor Roosevelt even planted a victory garden on the White House lawn. The Victory Garden campaign served as a successful means of boosting morale, expressing patriotism, safeguarding against food shortages on the home front, and easing the burden on commercial farmers.

In 1942, roughly 15 million families planted victory gardens. By 1944, an estimated 20 million victory gardens produced roughly 8 million tons of food, more than 40 percent of all the fresh fruits and vegetables consumed in the United States. The scientist, George Washington Carver, was born a slave in Diamond, Missouri. Carver's insatiable appetite for learning and his intellect led him to become one of America's most famous agricultural scientists. He invented over 300 products, including crop rotation. He became the head of Tuskegee College's Department of Agriculture in 1910 and educated poor farmers through movable schools. He wrote *"Nature's Garden for Victory and Peace," Bulletin No. 43,* printed in 1942. His thesis functioned as a manual that helped promote and develop the Victory Gardens of World War II and today's concept of fresh foods. [92] [93]

---

92   https://www.history.com/news/americas-patriotic-victory-gardens

93   https://henderson.ces.ncsu.edu/2020/04/george-washington-carvers-natures-garden-for-victory-and-peace-pamphlet-1942/

WACS

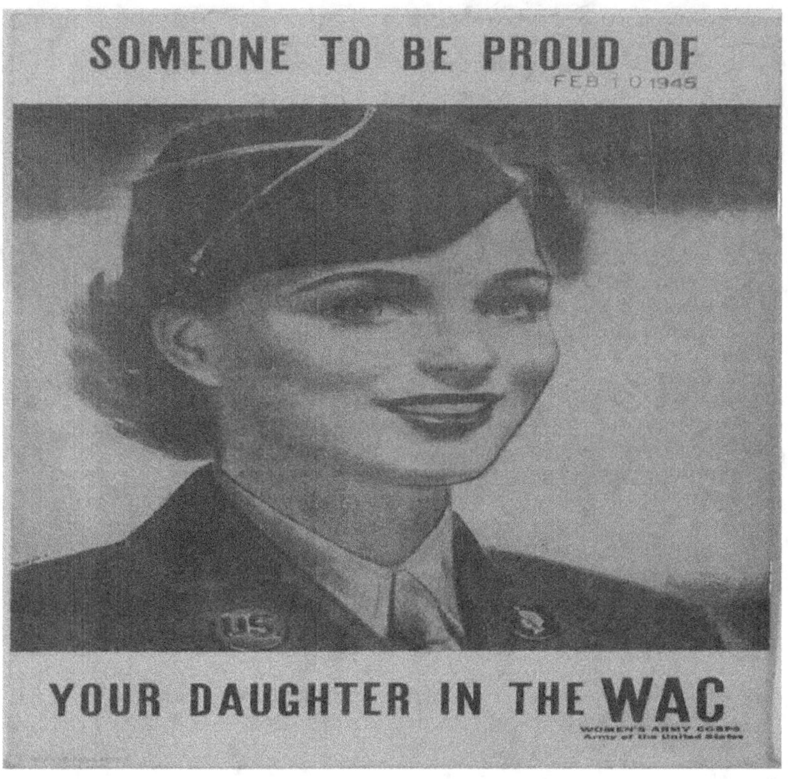

The Army had female support as nurses and others, but they created a formal unit for women to serve in 1942 as an auxiliary unit, and later in 1943 as an active duty unit. In World War II, 150,000 women enlisted. In 1978, women were integrated into the whole Army. From the beginning, Black women were admitted to the WACs on a ten percent ratio. Black women were also part of the Women's Army Auxiliary Corps (WAAC). From 1942, Black women had to follow the percentage recruitment limitations that matched the proportion of the black population.

Unfortunately, Black women experienced segregation and discrimination. There was a strike by the black WACS in World War II, and the court martial of four of them, Mary Green, Anna Morrison, Johnnie Murphy and Alice Young. The strike was a protest against racial and gender discrimination in the Army. They were charged and found guilty of disobeying an order of a superior officer. Thurgood Marshall, Congress, and the community demanded an investigation of their jail sentences. When they won the appeal and were reinstated, the Army conceded that it had not followed protocol. [94] [95]

---

94   www.britannica.com/topic/Womens-Army-Corps#:~

95   https://www.womensmemorial.org/history-of-black-women#:~:text=From%20its%20beginning

CELEBRATION GLASSES

Glasses c 1940s

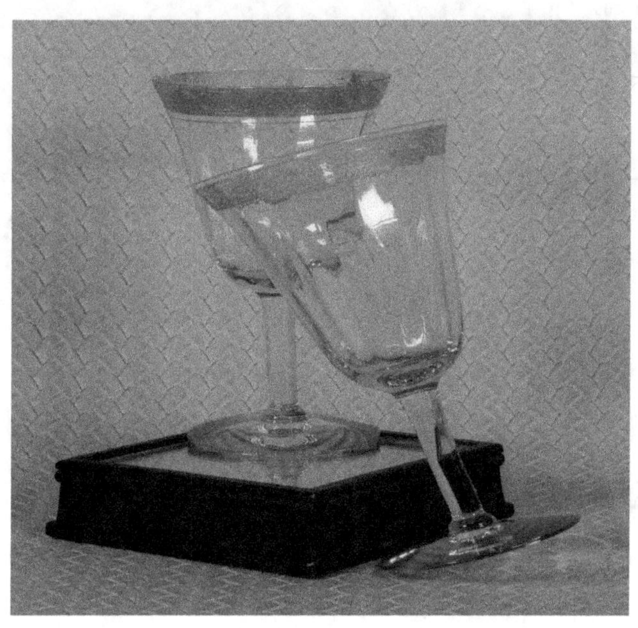

History earns its importance from our need to learn about the past, and honor that knowledge by using it to place the present and the future in proper perspective for the betterment of the human race. Thanks to new methods of analyzing items from the past, as learnt in Harvard University's courses, we can now take an object from a specific time, address its social implications, and use that data for our current situation. Museums can be places of fun, learning, community support, jobs, or Veterans outreach for morale-building service. We thank all those the people who were Acting On Hope during World War II. They are veritable role models for our today.

PUERTO RICAN VETERANS

The Boringueneers Veterans Receive The Congressional Gold Medal on June 10, 2014.

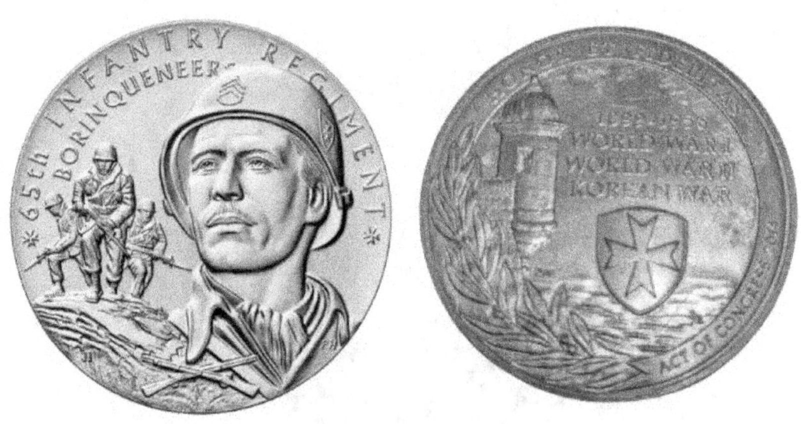

The Congressional Gold Medal is one of the highest awards the United States bestows. It is given as national appreciation for distinguished contributions. Only a handful of military units have ever received this award, and only one other Hispanic American has received it, Roberto Clemente, the Baseball Hall-of-Famer who died in a plane crash during an off-season humanitarian mission.

The Borinqueneers Veterans from Puerto Rico were awarded for their extraordinary service during World War II and the Korean War. The Congressional Gold Medal is 90 percent gold and worth about $3,600, but the honor is priceless. An original medal was given to ACES Veterans Museum by Latin American Post 840 on May 28, 2022. It was the 21st year of the Day of Honor for Black and Minority World Wa II Veterans at ACES Museum.

Manuel Lorenzo, the first Hispanic Commandant, and a decorated World War II Veteran, was the founding father of ACES. This original Medal will continue to preserve his legacy, and the legacy of Puerto Rican Veterans of WWII.

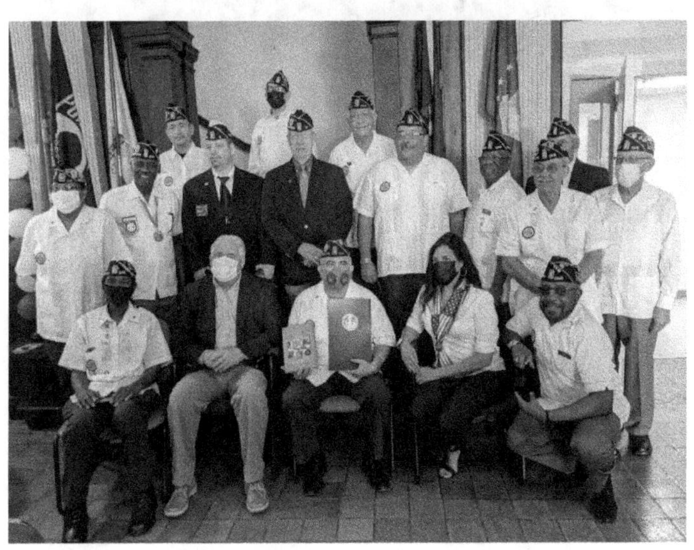

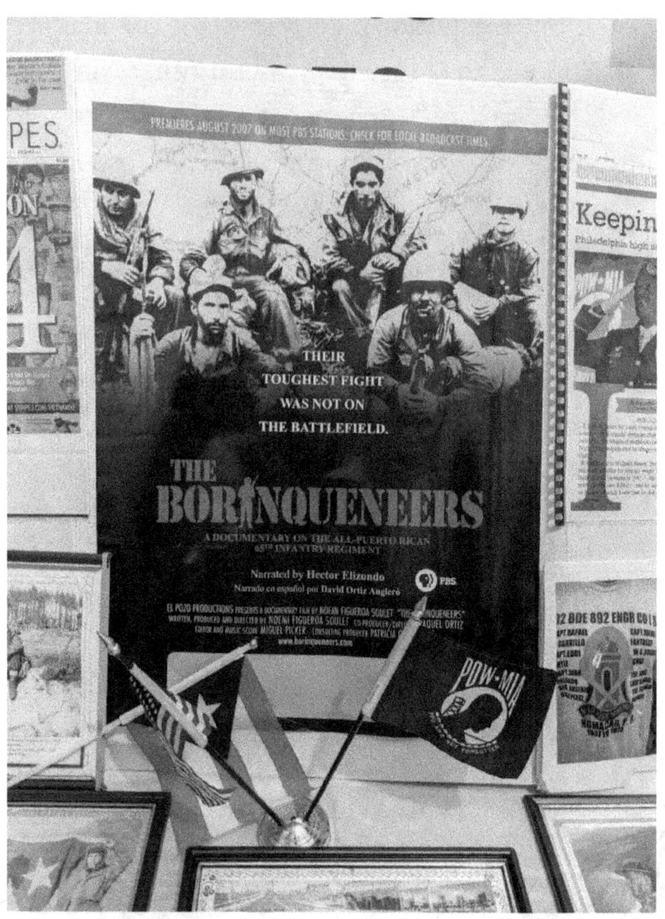

96   https://www.npr.org/sections/codeswitch/2014/05/23/315130878/
congress-to-award-highest-honor-to-armys-only-latino-unit

97   https://www.nationalguard.mil/News/Article/575821/puerto-ricos-65th-
infantry-regiment-receives-

VINTAGE

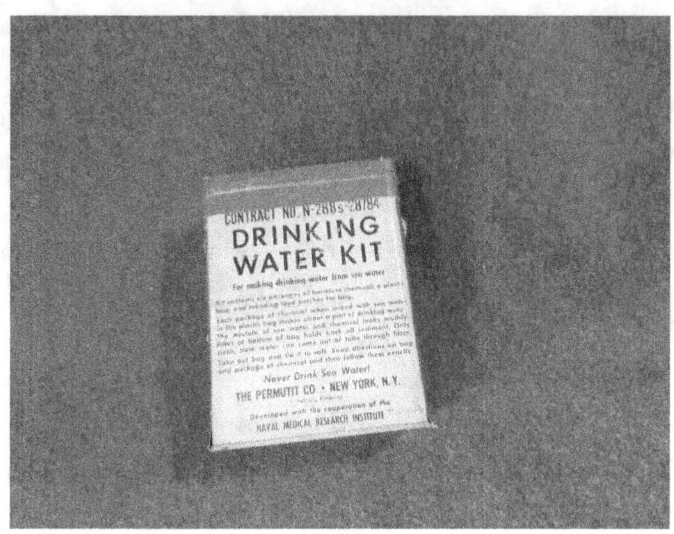

Water is an absolute necessity for soldiers and other physically active people. Water cools the body through perspiration. Over 60 percent of body weight is water, and dehydration can prove fatal if not quickly addressed, which is why water must be replaced as soon as it is lost in significant amounts.

Safe drinking water has been a concern throughout history. The oldest bottled water plant is the Holy Well in Malvern, England, and merchants have bottled and sold water there since 1622. The Holy Well has a natural spring and visitors often travel long distances to bathe in and drink the spring water.

Cargo ships of old obtained fresh drinking water through several sources, depending on their design, the route traveled, and the duration of the voyage. Modern ships are often equipped with onboard desalination plants that convert seawater to potable water using processes like reverse osmosis.

When injected into the water supply, chlorine will kill microbes. Beginning in 1895, Germany and Britain experimented with chlorination. Soon chlorination became a standard means of controlling water-borne disease. In World War II, *drinking water kits* typically referred to portable kits containing water purification tablets or chemicals that soldiers could use to treat potentially contaminated water sources like rivers or streams, allowing them to safely drink the water by killing harmful bacteria and parasites present in it, essentially making the water potable.

Soldiers had several ways to address contaminated water. Most commonly, there were clean water kits that contained iodine or chlorine-based tablets that were added to water to disinfect it. There were Lister bags, which were canvas bags that were designed to hold treated water. Field purification units were used to filter and purify water on a larger scale for entire units.

From World War II through the post-Vietnam era, the water purification process underwent only minimal change. Engineer water purification units set up operations near a stream or other acceptable water point. If the stream was too shallow, a few explosives could easily create a pond. Water was processed through the Erdlator, a field water treatment device developed during World War II during at the US Army's United States Army Engineer Research and Development Laboratory at Fort Belvoir, Virginia. In exceptional cases, a well was dug.

There are other drinking water considerations. Avoid using rainwater for drinking, cooking, brushing the teeth, or rinsing or watering plants intended for cooking.

Freshly melted snow is not safe for drinking purposes. Exercise caution with melted ice as you would for standing water, and if in doubt boil the water for ten minutes.

Seawater is not safe. While humans can safely ingest small amounts of salt, the salt content of seawater is much higher than what can be processed by the human body. It is decidedly unsafe to drink ocean water even if it is boiled. Boiling can kill bacteria and viruses, but it will not eliminate the high salt and mineral content of seawater. Consuming too much salt can lead to dehydration, kidney damage, and other health problems. An adequate dietary intake of water is about 15.5 cups (3.7 liters) of fluids a day for men, and about 11.5 cups (2.7 liters) of fluids a day for women. [98] [99] [100]

98   https://www.reddit.com/r/history/comments/3qzx9k/how_soldiers_have_obtained_and_treated_water_on/?rdt=47289

99   https://quartermaster.army.mil/qm_fuctional_areas/Potable_Water.pdf

100   https://www.health.harvard.edu/staying-healthy/how-much-water-should-you-drink

BRAVO

Military Footlocker

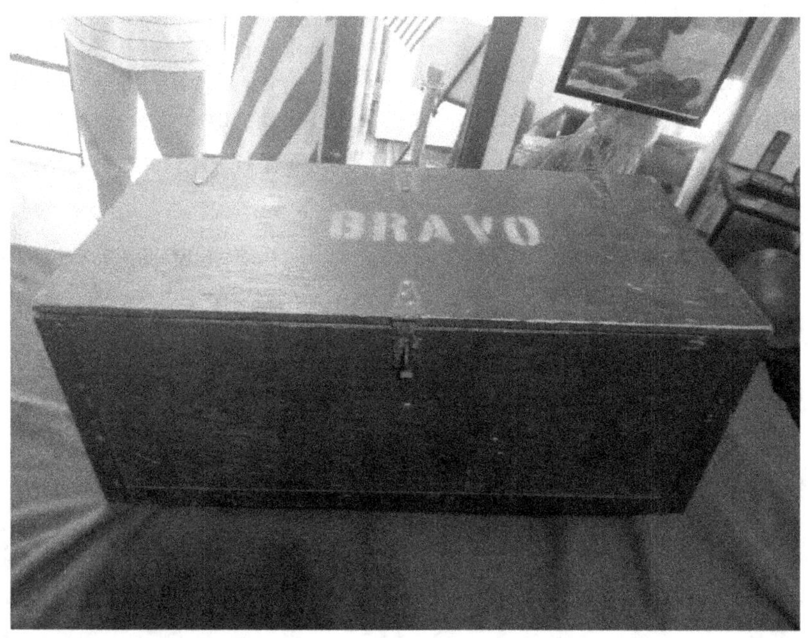

Footlockers are cuboid storage trunks, secured by a padlock or combination lock, and used by military personnel to store their personal belongings, equipment, and sundry other items. They are typically kept at the foot of a soldier's bed or bunk, which is where the term "footlocker" comes from. Although these storage field bins were widely used from 1939-1945 during World War II, the term "footlocker" is currently used in recruit training in the United States Marine Corps.

This footlocker is from BRAVO Company from the estate of a Private who served in World War II. Bravo Company is identified at 327 infantry, the infantry unit that worked with the 101 Airborne Division. The company's motto was, "For honor and Country," and they participated in multiple operations during WW II. One particularly significant maneuver was The Battle of the Bulge. The first

legally sanctioned integrated military maneuver, the Battle of the Bulge, also known as the Ardennes Offensive, was the last major German offensive. The Allies won the Battle of the Bulge, resulting in significantly higher casualties on the German side despite their surprise attack on Allied forces. Losing 120,000 people and military supplies, German forces were dealt an irreparable blow, while the Allied forces suffered only 75,000 casualties.

Black people served in various areas, including the 767th battalion. They also worked with the 103rd infantry division. There were also a 600th and a 14th tank destroyer battalions. The Black Panthers would go on to receive a presidential citation for bravery. Lt. Gen. George S. Patton, U.S. Third Army commander, awarded the Silver Star to Private Ernest A. Jenkins of New York City. He was a member of the 767th Tank Battalion.

The 787 Tank Battalion motto was, "It will be done." Because of the massive cop casualties and the German infiltration during the Battle of the Bulge, it was necessary to integrate on a comprehensive scale. German soldiers would not fight next to Black soldiers even though they could emulate white soldiers in multiple ways. Benjamin Barry, a board member of ACES Museum, was an original participant in the Battle of the Bulge, and his video is featured on YouTube. [101] [102]

---

101   https://www.nationalww2museum.org/war/articles/black-panthers-761st-tank-battalion-battle-of-the-bulge

102   n.m.wikipedia.org/wiki/File:"Lt._Gen._George_S._Patton,_U.S._Third_Army_commander,_pins_the_Silver_Star_on_Private_Ernest_A._Jenkins_of_New_York_Cit_-_NARA_-_5

POSTER

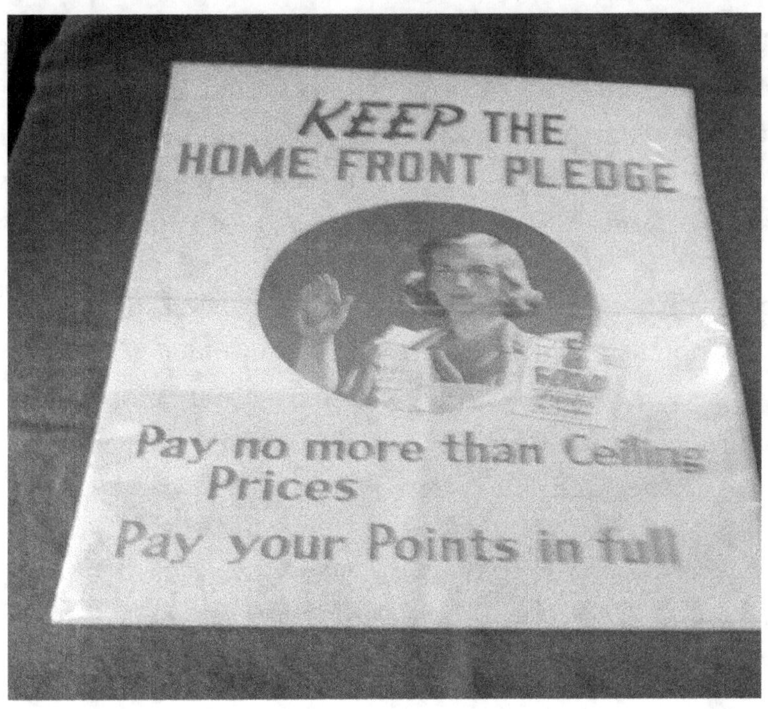

The original poster reflects the need for the public to assist in an effective war effort. During World War II, American civilians played a vital role on the "home front" by contributing to the war effort through rationing, working in factories to produce war materials, growing "Victory Gardens" to supplement food supplies, collecting scrap metal and other resources, and participating in civil defense measures like air raid warden programs.

There were other challenges like shortages of goods and the internment of Japanese Americans living in the U.S. Many Americans volunteered for Civilian Defense to defend the nation from enemy bombing or invasion. They trained in first aid, aircraft spotting, bomb removal, and firefighting. Air raid wardens led practice drills, including blackouts. Over 10 million Americans were civil defense volunteers by 1942.

There were shortages of cars, toys, fridges, and doctors and nurses. The government rationed food and gasoline. People across the country grew their own food and collected needed materials to support the war effort. George Washington Carver wrote the *"Nature's Garden for Victory and Peace"* Pamphlet in 1942.

Faced with the burden of feeding an expanded military and a hungry population, the US government reintroduced the concept of *War Gardens* from World War I. They rebranded them as *Victory Gardens* for World War II and spelled out their purpose with assistance from the Nature's Garden.

The Victory Garden Program would promote: Our Food Is Fighting: A Garden Will Make Your Rations Go Further." Poster, Office of War Information, 1943. Aims were to:

1. *Increase the production and consumption of fresh vegetables and fruits by more and better home, school, and community gardens, to the end that we become a stronger and healthier Nation.*

2. *Encourage the proper storage and preservation of the surplus from such gardens for distribution and use by families producing it, local school lunches, welfare agencies, and for local emergency food needs.*

3. *Enable families and institutions to save on the cost of vegetables and*

apply this saving to other necessary foods which must be purchased.

4. *Provide through the medium of community gardens, an opportunity for gardening by urban dwellers and others who lack suitable home garden facilities.*

5. *Maintain and improve the morale and spiritual well-being of the individual, family, and Nation. The beautification of the home and community by gardening provides healthful physical exercise, recreation, definite release from war stress and strain.*

-- (Garden for Victory: Guide for Planning the Local Victory Garden Program 1942) [1]

During World War II, Victory Gardens are estimated to have fed roughly half of all American families, with around 20 million gardens planted across the country, producing roughly 40% of the nation's fresh vegetables, and effectively feeding a significant portion of the US population.

George Washington Carver, who authored the *"Nature's Garden for Victory and Peace"* Pamphlet in 1942, was at the Tuskegee Institute in Alabama. He was a scientist with a Masters of Science in Agriculture and did his part to help people feed themselves. Born a slave in Diamond, Missouri, Carver's insatiable appetite for learning and understanding eventually led him to become a premier scientist. As the head of Tuskegee College's Department of Agriculture, he spent 33 years educating poor farmers through 'movable schools,' a predecessor to the modern County Extension Service, and other innovative programs.

Carver's inventions include hundreds of products, including more than 300 from peanuts (milk, plastics, paints, dyes, cosmetics, medicinal oils, soap, ink, and wood stains), 118 from sweet potatoes (molasses, postage stamp glue, flour, vinegar, and synthetic rubber), and even a type of gasoline. With his multiple inventions, he contributed tremendously to America's health, beyond the Victory Gardens. [103] [104] [105] [106]

---

103   https://www.nps.gov/articles/000/the-american-home-front-and-world-war-ii.htm#:~:text=Goods%20like%20cars%2C%20toys%2C%20and,materials%20to%20support%20the%20war

104   https://henderson.ces.ncsu.edu/2020/04/george-washington-carvers-natures-garden-for-victory-and-peace-pamphlet-1942/

105   https://www.nps.gov/articles/000/the-american-home-front-and-world-war-ii.htm#:~:text=Goods%20like%20cars%2C%20toys%2C%20and,materials%20to%20support%20the%20war.

106   https://www.nps.gov/articles/000/victory-gardens-on-the-world-war-ii-home-front.htm

WAVES

Miniature Uniform

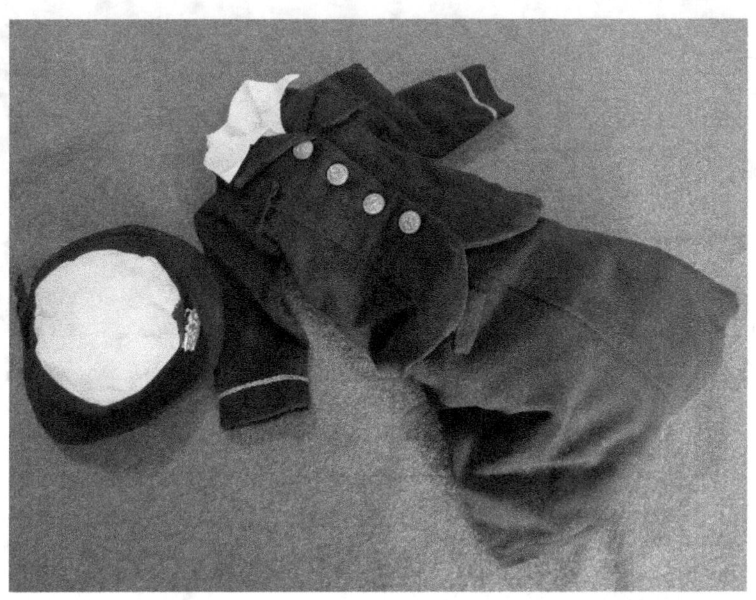

WAVES is acronym for *"Women Accepted for Volunteer Emergency Service."* WAVES was a World War II-era division of the United States Navy created in 1942. WAVES enabled women to serve in the Navy during wartime, filling critical support roles and freeing up male personnel for combat duties. Most especially, it freed up male sailors for combat duty by having women take on administrative and support roles on land.

WAVES was established on July 30, 1942, by President Franklin D. Roosevelt as the first women's military organization in the US Navy. Initially, WAVES were restricted to shore duty, but later served on ships and in hospitals, with about 100,000 women serving in WAVES during World War II.

Their roles included clerical and administrative work, communications and cryptography, intelligence and analysis, medical and healthcare support, and technical and scientific work. A notable fact about WAVES, whose uniforms and ranks were similar to those of male Navy personnel, was their prohibition from serving in combat or flying aircraft. Although WAVES was disbanded in 1946, it paved the way for future women's military service in the United States.

The WAVES program recruited women between 18 and 36 years old, and officers between 20 and 50 years old, to serve onshore in the continental United States. Many of these women, starting in 1944, also served in Alaska and Hawaii. WAVES worked at 900 locations in America. Public law 689 prohibited them from serving on ships or overseas, although that law was later amended. Many WAVES personnel worked in clerical, health care, and storekeeper billets. Approximately 14,000 of them served as yeomen, while another 13,000 served as hospital corpsmen. The women also served as codebreakers for the Office of Naval Operations' highly secretive Communications Division in Washington, DC.

WAVES personnel were assigned to aviation units to maintain aircraft, test parachutes, and serve as domestic air traffic controllers and weather specialists, while also training male celestial navigators in navigation and gunnery. Out of the over 90,000 women who served in WAVES at enlisted and officer rank levels, most were white; comprising only two officers, and 70 enlisted women were African American because the Navy only began to recruit them late in the war's progression.

Hospital Apprentices Second Class Ruth C. Isaacs, Katherine Horton, and Inez Patterson were the first Black WAVES to enter the Hospital Corps School at National Naval Medical Center in Bethesda, Maryland. Hospital Apprentices were enlisted medical specialists who served as the primary medical caregivers for sailors. They also served as assistants in the prevention and treatment of disease and injuries.

The WAVES left a remarkable legacy. They proved women's capabilities in military service. They opened the doors for future generations of women in the Navy and other branches of the United States Armed Forces, and they contributed significantly to the war effort and Allied victory. Ultimately, the WAVES program was a groundbreaking step towards gender equality in the US military, demonstrating women's value and dedication to serving their country.

Notable WAVES included Captain Joy Bright Hancock, first woman to receive the Navy's Legislative Liaison Award, Lieutenant Commander Dorothy C. Stratton, first director of WAVES, and Ensign Harriet Ida Pickens, one of the first African American women to join WAVES. [107] [108] [109]

---

107   https://www.history.navy.mil/browse-by-topic/diversity/women-in-the-navy/waves.html

108   https://rediscovering-black-history.blogs.archives.gov/2015/03/10/pictorial-history-of-black-women-in-the-us-navy-during-world-war-ii-and-beyond/

109   https://airandspace.si.edu/stories/editorial/waves-program-color-world-war-2

THE MARINE DEVIL DOG

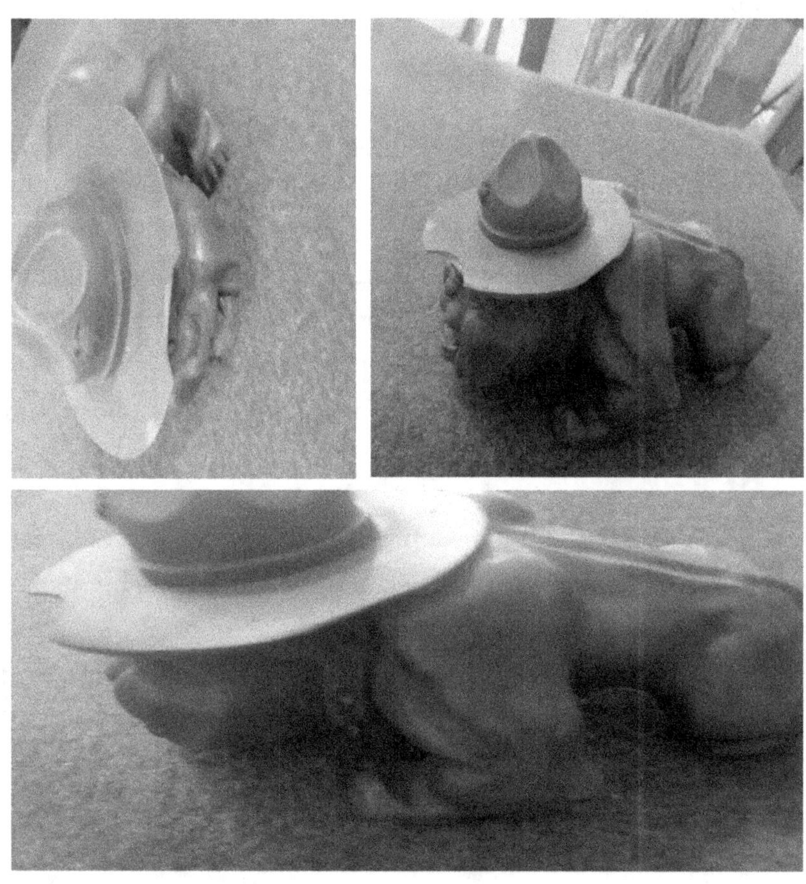

The *"Devil Dog"* moniker is principally associated with the Marine Corps' mascot, a bulldog named *Chesty*, named after legendary Marine Corps General Lewis "Chesty" Puller. That English bulldog has represented the Marines as a mascot since 1922, although the first bulldog to serve as mascot was *Jiggs*, who entered the Marine Corps as a Private in early 1922. The image of a bulldog wearing a Marine Corps helmet on recruiting posters helped establish the bulldog as the mascot.

The *"Marine Devil Dog"* is a nickname for members of the United States Marine Corps, particularly those who have earned the title through their bravery and toughness. The term *"Devil Dog"* originated during World War I, when German soldiers referred to Marines as *"Teufelhunde,"* meaning *"Devil Dogs,"* due to their ferocity and tenacity in combat. The term has since become an iconic symbol of Marine Corps culture and esprit de corps, representing the values of *ferocity*; unrelenting combat spirit and willingness to fight, *tenacity*; unwavering commitment to mission and comrades, *loyalty*; unshakeable dedication to the Corps and fellow Marines, and *pride;* unapologetic swagger and confidence in their abilities. The Marine Devil Dog represents the epitome of Marine Corps spirit and tradition, inspiring Marines to live up to the high standards of their predecessors and earn the revered title.

Dogs were recruited as part of the World War II effort. A coalition called *Dogs for Defense, Inc. (DFD)* encouraged dog owners all across the country to donate their dogs for training as sentry dogs, while the American Kennel Club supported the procurement of dogs. On July 16, 1942, Secretary of War, Henry L. Stimson, issued a directive that assigned responsibility for procuring and training dogs to the Remount Branch of the Quartermaster Corps (QMC) and expanded their mandate to include the training of dogs for both sentry duty and possible tactical missions as well.

By June 1944, the War Department had authorized the creation of fifteen Quartermaster war dog platoons. These units had their own Table of Organization and Equipment that included eighteen scout dogs, sixteen messenger dogs, twenty enlisted men, and one officer. All fifteen platoons were shipped overseas by the end of the year; seven to Europe and eight to the Pacific. For the invasion of the Philippines, the 25th, 26th, 39th, 40th, 41st, and 43d Quarter Master War Dog Platoons were attached to various infantry units. By this time, the effectiveness of the dogs had been well established and there were not enough to go around for all the units that requested them for their patrols. The dogs were invaluable in the jungle warfare that characterized much of the combat the Pacific Theater. Dogs provided part of the tactical puzzle to engage the Japanese in the jungles.

After the war, the Marines ensured that the dogs had homes. ACES Veterans Museum sponsored a *Puppets with History Program* called *Rockett the Dog that Saves Colors* at Gettysburg WWII Reenactment which taught about the Marines' Devil Dogs. Rockett wanted to join to save "colors." but she was handicapped by the insecurity that attended being called "Bad." [110] [111]

---

110   https://www.6thmarines.marines.mil/Units/1st-Battalion/History/#:~:text=Devil%20Dog,up%20it%20on%20all%20fours.

111   https://armyhistory.org/the-dogs-of-war-the-u-s-armys-use-of-canines-in-wwii/

SPY CAMERAS AND ORGANIZED NETWORKS

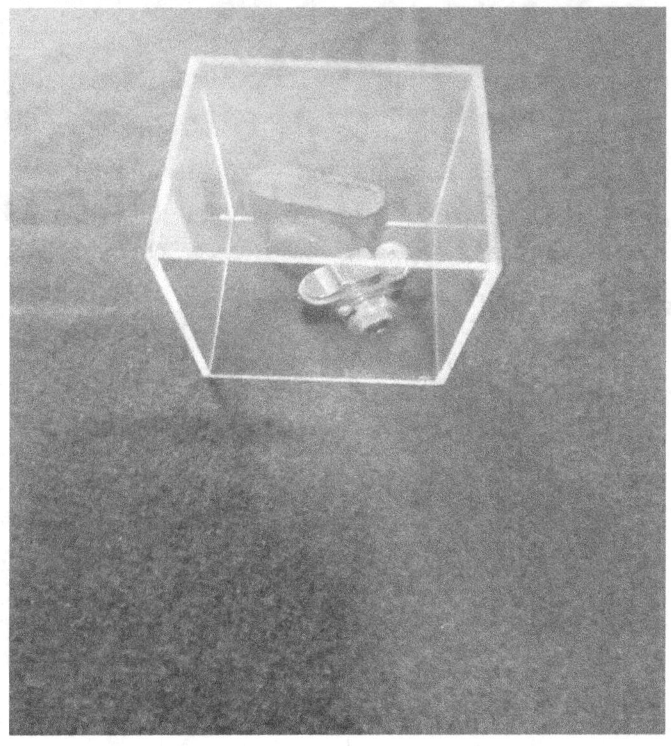

The Spy camera's close-focusing lens and small size made it perfect for covert uses such as surveillance or document copying. Small cameras were used by both the Axis and Allies. Some of the cameras were used by pigeons to take aerial shots. A device was fitted to the breast of the pigeon and they flew over the target. Eastern Kodak also produced a camera that was so small it could fit into a matchbox. He would go on to be famous for Kodak films. These small cameras were used by the US OSS, Office of Strategic Services during World War II.

Office of Strategic Services, was the first independent intelligence agency and it was formed in 1942. It only lasted for three years but it would become the basis for the CIA. Noteworthy women of the OSS included Virginia Hall who used her artificial leg to help create a spy network and organize French commandos. She received the Distinguished Service Cross. Also, a member of the OSS was Marlena Dietrich who received the Medal of Freedom because of her work with helping the United States with morale. She became an American citizen.

The OSS, Office of Special Services, was the British special operatives executive branch of the military. Its goal was to organize and perform intelligence espionage and sabotage.

Women that are noteworthy for their roles in the OSS particularly Maria Koshetz Gulovich was recruited and eventually won a Bronze Star for bravery. Gertrude Stanford who from South Carolina who also was awarded the Bronze Star.

Noor Inayat Khan was the 1st radio operative for the French Resistance from the OSS. In 1943 she helped 30 allied airmen escape. She was awarded did George Cross, the highest civilian award of the United Kingdom.

Josephine Baker was an internationally known member of the French Resistance. Known as an entertainer, she was one of the first black women to get her pilot's license. She was a friend of Bessie Coleman who was the first black female to get her Flyers license in 1921. She had gone to France in order to fly and met Ms. Baker. Josephine Baker was to use her pilot's license to fly her own airplane to transport supplies for the Red Cross and for the French resistance. In addition to providing supplies, Josephine Baker also used her own finances and jewels to help to feed the hungry in France.

As an intricate part of the resistance movement, she used her notoriety to get intelligence as she performed around the world during the war.

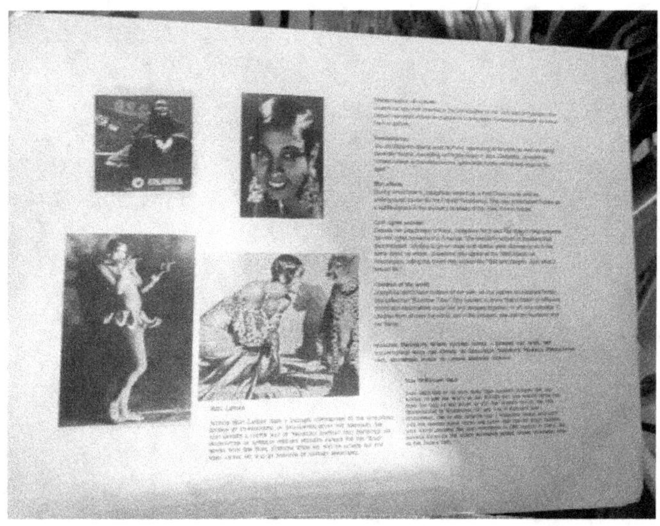

French Airforce Lieutenant Josephine Baker was so diligent in her dedication that even upon recovery from multiple surgeries, she was participating in the spy network and helping to distribute information to the allied forces.

Her nicknames included Siren of Resistance and Creole Goddess for the work that she did with the French Resistance and the OSS. After the war she was awarded the Croix de Guerre, the "War Cross" of valor in combat, the highest honor of France.

---

112   https://www.cia.gov/stories/story/josephine-baker-from-poverty-to-stardom-to-espionage/

113   https://www.britannica.com/topic/Office-of-Strategic-Services

114   ia.gov/stories/story/glorious-amateurs-of-oss-sisterhood-of-spies/

115   https://guides.loc.gov/french-resistance-world-war-two/women-in-the-french-resistance

116   https://www.history.com/news/josephine-baker-world-war-ii-spy

117   https://www.shttps://guides.loc.gov/french-resistance-world-war-two/women-in-the-french-resistance

ERVIN ODOM - CONGRESSIONAL GOLD MEDAL

The Montford Point Marines

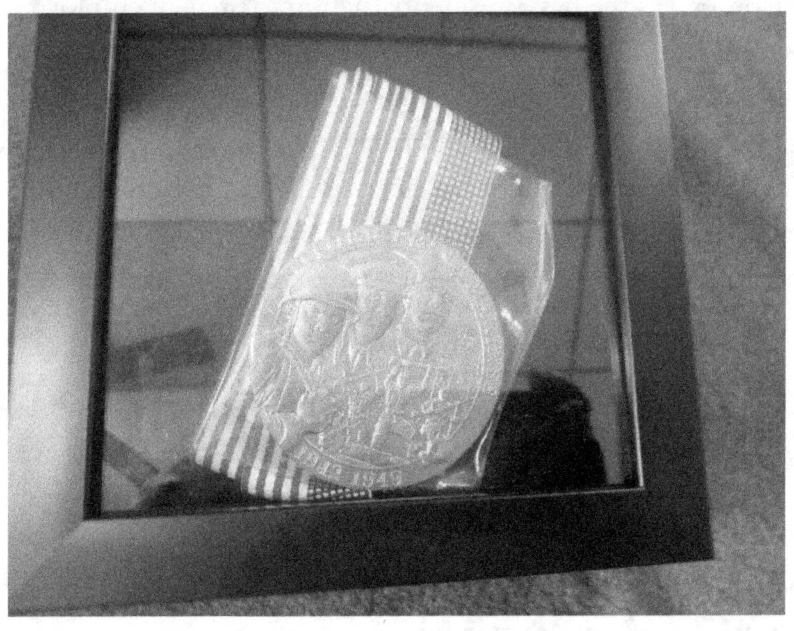

Although the Marine Corps was founded in 1775, Blacks would not be allowed enlistment into this elite corps until 1941. In that year, 1941, the United States was preparing to enter World War II, and it needed recruits. But President Franklin D. Roosevelt faced a problem. Racial discrimination was still the norm in the armed forces, but civil rights leaders were organizing for change, and there was intense pressure for a reluctant Roosevelt to open up the defense industry to blacks. However, under pressure from his wife, Eleanor, Roosevelt conceded, and on June 25, 1941, the president signed Executive Order 8802, prohibiting racial discrimination in the defense industry or in government.

Executive Order 8802 read, *"There is evidence that available and needed workers have been barred from employment in industries engaged in defense production solely because of considerations of race, creed, color, or national origin, to the detriment of workers' morale and of national unity."*

The order was the first presidential action to prevent employment discrimination by private employers with government contracts. It also established the Fair Employment Practices Committee (FEPC) to investigate incidents of discrimination. In essence, the order was an important step toward eliminating racial discrimination in the U.S. defense industry and in federal government employment practices. It also helped Black Americans find jobs as skilled workers in cities like Detroit, Baltimore, and Indianapolis.

The Montford Point Marines came into existence in June 1941 from Executive Order 8802. Blacks were allowed to join the Marine Corp after that Executive Order but, they were trained at a segregated base at Montfort Point, North Carolina. They distinguished themselves during service. The African American Marines served with distinction.

One incident was the Battle of Peleliu. In one of the most bitter battles the Marines faced during World War II, a platoon of African American Marines fought their way to capture an airstrip and save a company of embattled white Marines. The Montford Point Marines, also known as the *"Forgotten Warriors,"* were named after the segregated Montford Point training camp in North Carolina.

They faced multiple challenges. These brave men faced racism through denial of their promotions and a refusal to recognize their valiant efforts. As the war progressed, however, and with increasing need for fighting men, the Montford Point Marines were finally given the opportunity to fight alongside their white counterparts. They proved themselves to be skilled and dedicated Marines, earning the respect and admiration of their peers. In 1945, Frederick C. Branch would be the first Black Marine commissioned officer. Over 12,000 Black Marines served overseas during WWII. These Marines served in Okinawa and in China during World War II. They would also serve in Korea and Vietnam.

The Montford Point Marines later received the highest civilian honor in the United States. President Barack Obama signed legislation to award these Marines the Congressional Gold Medal in November 2011. This honor is awarded to individuals who have significantly contributed to American history and culture. The Montford Point Marines certainly fit this criteria, as they served their country honorably, paving the way for future generations of African Americans in the military.

We are proud to disclose that the estate of Montford Point Marine, Ervin Odom, donated his Congressional Gold Medal to ACES Veterans Museum. [118] [119] [120]

---

118   Britannica.com/event/Executive-Order-8802

119   ejeune.marines.mil/Portals/27/Documents/EMD/Cultural-Resources/PublicOutreach/Montford%20Point%20Display1.pdf

120   ationalww2museum.org/war/articles/men-montford-point-and-good-war

ORIGINAL MARINE PAINTING

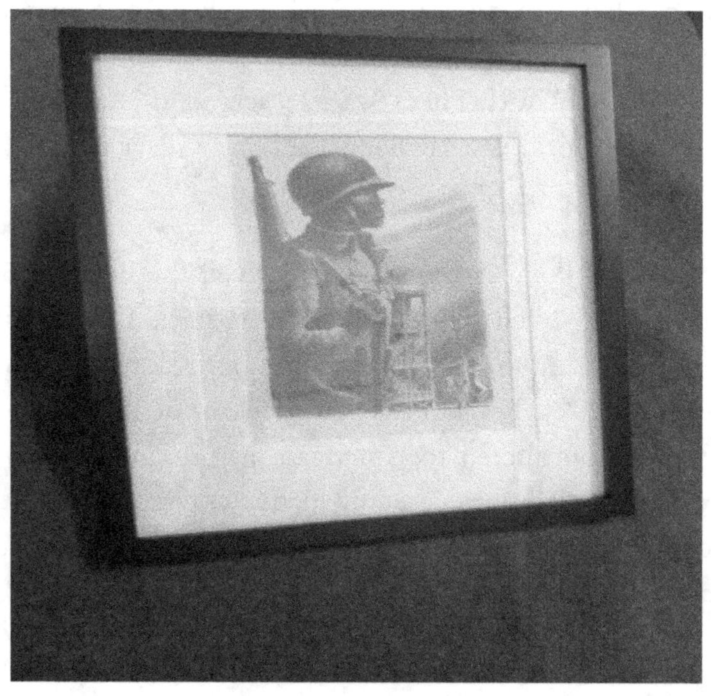

This painting was produced during World War II to honor Black people who served in the Marines. Integration into the United States Marine Corps encountered daunting challenges but, in good faith, the Black men entered Montfort Point camp in North Carolina for segregated training and became Marines.

These African American marines were the first to serve in the Marine Corps since the 1796 law that outlawed discrimination based on race and sex in recruitment into the defense forces. The Emancipation Proclamation of 1863 allowed Black people into the Army but not the Marines.

Initially, there was widespread sentiment that Black people would not be able to perform in the Marines due to the complexity of the training. This view was vehemently challenged by A. Philip Randolph and other Civil Rights activists. Civil Rights leaders planned a march on Washington with over 100,000 participants to point out the hypocrisy of the United States in fighting for freedom and human rights overseas, but not allowing Blacks to enjoy the same equal rights and dignity at home.

President Roosevelt, on the eve of the March on Washington, finally agreed to sign Executive Order 8802, which he did on June 25, 1941, eliminating discrimination in employment in the federal government of the United States. President Roosevelt was said to be concerned about the embarrassment the United States would suffer from the Axis powers, as well as possible race riots, were blacks not allowed equal rights.

Black Marine combat support units also took part in the assault on Iwo Jima, and Peleliu. Their presence forced "accidental integration," since there was a random intermingling of white and black units. Ten days after Iwo Jima was declared secure, the Japanese launched a final attack that penetrated to the rear area units near Iwo Jima᾿s western beaches, including the 8th Ammunition and 36th Marine Depot Companies. The Black Marines helped stop the enemy. Two members of the 36th Company, Privates James M. Whitlock and James Davis, earned the Bronze Star for «heroic achievement." The African-American companies that fought at Iwo Jima shared in the Navy Unit Citation awarded the support units of V Amphibious Corps.

In total, 19,168 African Americans joined the Marines, about 4% of the USMC›s strength, with some 75% of them performing their duties overseas. About 8,000 Black USMC stevedores and ammunition handlers served under enemy fire during offensive operations in the Pacific.

In 1945 the first Black officer of the United States Marines was Second Lieutenant Fred C. Branch in 1949. Annie N. Graham was the first African-American woman to join the United States Marine Corps, serving from 1949 to 1952. Graham›s service came after the Women›s Armed Services Integration Act was passed in 1948, which permanently allowed women to serve in the Marine Corps. [121] [122]

---

121   https://www.nps.gov/parkhistory/online_books/npswapa/extcontent/usmc/pcn-190-003132-00/sec10.htm#:~:text=When%20the%201st%20Marine%20Division,Major%20General

122   https://www.marines.mil/Portals/1/Publications/Blacks%20in%20the%20Marine%20Corps%20%20PCN%2019000306200_1.pdf

BILLIE HOLIDAY'S "STRANGE FRUIT"

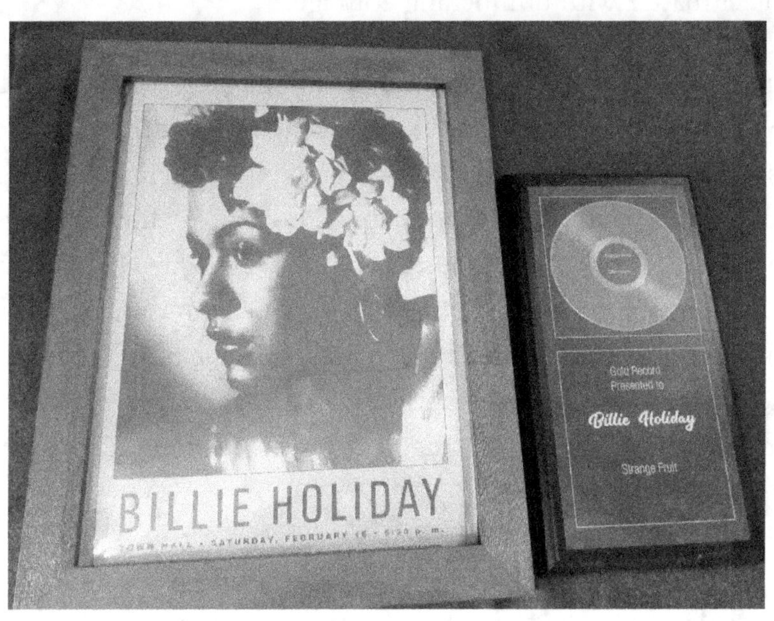

Billie Holiday was known for several things. She was an accomplished vocalist, international performer, and the first Black woman to sing with an all-white band. She also sang *"Strange Fruit,"* the powerful and haunting song written by Lewis Allan in 1937. The song is a poignant protest against racial violence, specifically lynching, in the American South. The lyrics describe the brutal scene of a lynching, with vivid imagery and metaphors.

Billie Holiday first performed *"Strange Fruit"* in 1939 at *Cafe Society*, a popular New York nightclub and hub for progressive politics and art. Her rendition was a defining moment in her career and cemented her status as a jazz legend. It is acknowledged that Billie Holiday's delivery of *"Strange Fruit"* was intensely *emotive* because she conveyed the song's raw emotion and outrage, authentically *intimate* because her voice created a sense of quiet, personal reflection, and profoundly *powerful* because she tackled the brutal subject matter with unflinching courage.

Expectedly, the song became a signature piece of sorts for Billie Holiday, and she performed it throughout her career. *"Strange Fruit"* has since become an iconic symbol of the Civil Rights Movement and a testament to the enduring impact of Billie Holiday's music artistry. Her version was inducted into the Grammy Hall of Fame in 1978, and although the song has been rendered by numerous other artists, Billie Holiday's version remains the most iconic, and it continues to move and inspire audiences, serving as a powerful reminder of the ongoing struggle for racial justice and equality.

Billie Holiday's song, *"Strange Fruit,"* rather starkly brought the tragedy of lynching into American consciousness in a manner that had not been seen since Ida B. Wells-Barnett published a pamphlet on lynching entitled *The Red Record,* in which she demonstrated statistically that the majority of lynching victims were men who had competed successfully against white-owned businesses.

Most agree that the courage Billie Holiday demonstrated in consistently rendering *"Strange Fruit"* through the years, despite its tragic symbolism, ought to accord her the status of a *"Mother of Civil Rights."* It should also totally overshadow her drug problems, if not even offering the explanation that her reliance on drugs was probably an escape outlet for the pressures that attended her refusal to deny a very negative aspect of life as a Black person. [123] [124] [125] [126]

---

123   https://billieholiday.com/

124   https://www.army.mil/article/233117/honoring_black_history_world_war_ ii_service_to_the_nation#:~:text=During%20WWII%2C%20more%20than%20 2.5,the%20Army%20during%20the%20

125   https://www.google.com/ search?q=women+in+world+war+2&rlz=1C1CHBF_ enUS894US894&oq=women+in+world+war+2&gs_lcrp=EgZjaHJvbWUyDggA EEUYORhDGIAEGIoFMgcIARAAGIAEMgcIAhAriking-women.org/module/ women-and-work/world-war-ii-1939-1945

126   https://www.history.com/topics/world-war-ii

DOUBLE VICTORY CAMPAIGN

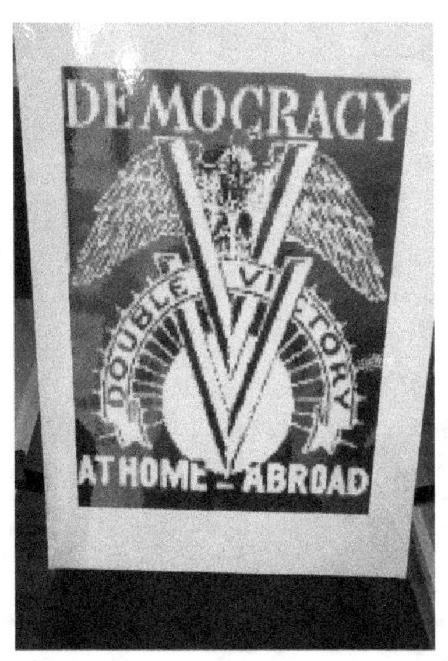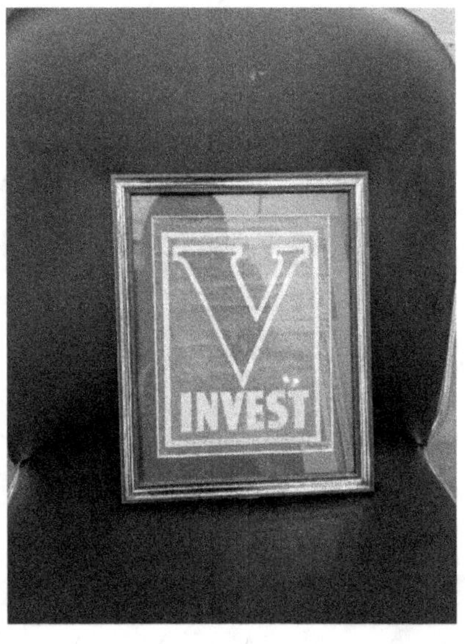

In 1942 the *Pittsburgh Courier*, an African American newspaper, launched the Double Victory Campaign, which stood for *"Victory Abroad and Victory at Home." Victory Abroad* championed military success against fascism overseas, and *Victory at Home* demanded equality for African Americans in the United States.

World War II started in the year 1939 with Germany's invasion of Poland. It was to last six bloody years until 1945 when the Allies defeated the Axis powers of Nazi Germany, Japan and Italy. Although World War II ended in 1945, the Civil Rights Movement continued to gain momentum well into the 1960s due to the participation of several World War II veterans who continued the

Double Victory Campaign. Such veterans Included, but were not limited to Meger Everts and Cesar Chavez, who were prominent in the organization of voter and worker rights.

Other WWII veterans would support racial equality through entertainment, including; Gene Roddenberry, Rod Sterling, Harry Belafonte, and Sidney Portier. Politicians who worked towards equality included Mayor Coleman Young, Senator Daniel Inouye and others. Audie Murphy would champion treatment for veterans with post-traumatic stress disorder, now known as *Invisible Wounds.*

Veterans and civilians worked hard to present and preserve the history of blacks and minorities during World War II. Their efforts deserve praise because maintaining a correct record keeps the true history from being obliterated, apart from preventing false narratives and biases based on sex or race. This is also important because racism can only continue to grow if there is only limited and prejudicial historical information.

In choosing to serve in the military, African Americans sought to have their service understood by the nation as a demand for liberty and citizenship. African American men and women who served in the military made their engagement useful, not only for the good of their country, but to benefit both their personal lives and their community, especially in the sustained fight for racial equality and justice. [127]

---

127 Double Victory | National Museum of African American History and Culture

ABOUT THE AUTHOR

A.V Hankins, MD FACP MPA M.Ed., is a medical doctor who has dedicated time and effort to the preservation of Parker Hall, a building facility that functioned as a Black USO during World War II.

She is the Founder and Director of ACES Veterans Museum, a preservation facility that seeks to honor Black and Minority Veterans and their Families. ACES Veterans Museum has locations in Philadelphia, Pennsylvania, and Pontiac, Michigan.

As a leading physician, and one of America's most eminent medical practitioners, Dr. Hankins has, over the decades, sustained her passion as an advocate for comprehensive medical and community care.

A certified *Veteran Ready* by PsychArmor, edh., she has also committed to a lifetime of unstinting devotion to the cause of America's Veterans through the invaluable work she is doing at ACES Veterans Museum.

www.ingramcontent.com/pod-product-compliance
Lightning Source LLC
Chambersburg PA
CBHW051742250726
48659CB00001B/194